Writing Skills for Education Students

www.thestudyspace.com – the leading study skills website

For a complete listing of all our titles in this area please visit
www.macmillanihe.com/study-skills

Writing Skills for Education Students

**Charlotte Barrow and
Rebecca Westrup**

First published 2019 by
RED GLOBE PRESS

Red Globe Press in the UK is an imprint of Springer Nature Limited,
registered in England, company number 785998, of 4 Crinan Street,
London N1 9XW.

Red Globe Press® is a registered trademark in the United States,
the United Kingdom, Europe and other countries.

ISBN 978–1–137–61018–8 paperback

This book is printed on paper suitable for recycling and made from fully
managed and sustained forest sources. Logging, pulping and manufacturing
processes are expected to conform to the environmental regulations of the
country of origin.

A catalogue record for this book is available from the British Library.

A catalog record for this book is available from the Library of Congress.

Contents

Introduction

This book is about how you can get the most out of your degree and develop and enhance your knowledge, understanding and skills required to be a successful Education student. Drawing on current students' experiences of studying an undergraduate Education degree programme and our experiences as lecturers, we hope the information from us and tips from our students will help you to feel prepared and confident about your studies. In this short introduction we consider what it means to be a student of Education and set out the aims of the book before explaining its structure.

What does it mean to be a student of Education?

The study of Education is interdisciplinary and draws on a number of subjects including Sociology, Psychology, History, Politics and Philosophy to develop our understanding and broaden our knowledge of how all ages learn, and the factors that can impact positively and negatively on this (Westrup, 2017). It also draws on wider aspects to critically explore the role of key facets such as society, the media and families. Education is a subject of importance to individuals, families, communities, governments and politicians, and society more broadly. The way in which we invest time and money in discussing and analysing the education system through debate and media coverage is indicative of the importance of education to the public interest.

Although throughout this book we refer primarily to 'Education' students, note that this text is also relevant to those studying on programmes in similar disciplines such as Childhood Studies, Early Years, Education and Social Care, or as an introductory text for students undertaking a Master's in Education if prior undergraduate study has been in a different discipline – learning to write in another academic field can make further study and professional development challenging, and so this book will support students in that position too.

So, what does it mean to be a student of Education? You'll find some more discussion around this in Chapter 5, but initially, it is useful for you to recognise that being a student of Education means that you are developing:

- Your curiosity and enquiry around the process of teaching and learning, and not just that which happens in the classroom.
- An interest in the educational experiences of learners from a wide variety of backgrounds, recognising that different opportunities and circumstances make educational successes and trajectories hugely variable.
- A reflective approach towards your own educational experiences, and ongoing way(s) of learning and developing yourself as a potential professional working in a field related to education.

Your own development as a successful learner will depend upon a wide range of experiences during your time as an Education student, including but not limited to:

- Detailed self-reflection upon your own educational experiences and destinations.
- Partnership with your peers to extend your own reflections and enable you to gain new understandings based on others' views.
- Commitment to engaging with the literature through extensive and purposeful research and reading.
- Analysis of 'facts', perspectives, experiences, data and other kinds of evidence to enable you to present informed and reasoned judgements on educational issues.
- Time spent immersed in educational settings whereby you can take on the role of observer and note and pursue lines of thought that link practice and theory.

All of these experiences and opportunities are not only to enable you to pass assessments and gain a qualification, but crucially they will help you become a more insightful and analytical thinker, evidenced in the way you interact with peers, future learners you might teach and also in the kinds of writing that you will be undertaking throughout your programme.

The scope of this book and how to use it in conjunction with your programme

Many undergraduate programmes addressing Education and the study of educational concepts and issues embed aspects of study skills into their modules, and every institution has slightly differing ideas about what is expected from students in terms of academic conventions, approaches and presentation of assessed work. This book isn't designed to act as a substitute for the advice and key information you will hear from your lecturers and tutors or what you will read about in module guides and course handbooks, but it can support you in the development of your key skills that will enable more efficient, less stressful and better organised approaches to study.

This book is divided into three parts. In Part I we explore a range of skills and approaches associated with information seeking skills, reading effectively and using sources appropriately with academic integrity. These are the foundations, the building blocks if you like, for becoming an Education student and successfully engaging in academic (and independent study).

Part II focuses on writing as an Education student. Within this section we establish some of the principles and approaches that apply to all kinds of assessment at university and then focus on a few common kinds of assignments that have particular characteristics to them. This section you can dip in and out of when faced with an impending assignment. One point to note is that we've used an informal tone in our writing so that the book is easily understandable. You shouldn't adopt such a writing style in your assignments, and in this section you will find some examples of academic-style writing and a focus on approaches and language to use to ensure your work is appropriately academic. We also look at feedback and discuss how you can learn from tutors' comments on your work during and after you've submitted your work.

In Part III the focus is on observation and reflection methods. These two skills are central to Education courses and critical reflection can provide a valuable starting point for creating future reflective practitioners.

It is our intention that this book will make you feel less apprehensive, and more empowered and informed, as a student of Education. And, while we sincerely hope that the advice and strategies in this book enable you to become a more successful learner and produce written assignments of a higher standard, our equal hope is that you enjoy and continue to love learning about the wonder of education throughout your life.

Becoming an Education Student

What Should I Be Reading?

It hopefully won't come as too much of a shock to you that a significant amount of your time spent studying your Education degree will involve *reading*. Traditionally, students referred to themselves as 'reading for a degree' – for example, 'I'm reading History' – or they might have been asked, 'What are you reading at university?' which would have meant, 'What are you *studying?*' While we no longer use this kind of language to refer to our studies, this once commonly used phrase is indicative of the fact that an enormous amount of time needs to be dedicated to reading. In fact, it is probably fair to say that this is the most essential component of studying Education at university. This means that you need to be prepared and well-informed about how to plan and manage your reading, so that you can do this most effectively.

This chapter:

- Focuses on the *kinds* of material that you might be reading within your Education degree.
- Will help you to develop an understanding of why some sources (pieces of reading) are more suitable than others.
- Introduces you to the nature and scope of educational research.
- Provides you with some information and tools to assess the credibility of the sources you use.

Why do we read?

This is not a trick question! Take a moment to think about the reasons *why* we need to read about a subject or an issue and see if you can note down three specific reasons in Activity 1.1.

ACTIVITY 1.1

Reasons to read as part of a degree programme

1 _____

_____

2 _____

_____

3 _____

_____

Some of your answers might have included the following reasons or ideas:

- To know 'facts' – for example, dates, names of theories or important people.
- To learn more detail or depth about a subject – for example, you may have a one-hour introductory lecture about a particular issue, and be asked to find out more about the finer details surrounding that topic.
- To help consolidate what we learn in lectures or other face-to-face sessions with lecturers – attending a lecture or seminar about a particular issue will provide you with some information, but reading after that session will help to reinforce new knowledge.
- To 'read around' an issue so that we understand other factors that might have influenced a particular educational development or event.
- To be able to identify where our ideas have come from when we include them in an assignment (see more about the importance of this in Chapter 2).
- To be aware of data or evidence that we might need to cite (refer to) in an academic piece of work – for example, you might need to include some up-to-date statistics on pupil attainment in an assignment.
- To gain an awareness and understanding of different perspectives – a class session may introduce you to particular points of view about an educational policy, theory or strategy, but if you read around this further, you'll learn that there are many more opinions, interpretations and perceptions to be considered.

This last point on the list above is important to anyone studying an academic subject at university but is particularly pertinent to you, as a student of Education. Education as a subject, or an important issue, is central to nearly all societies. Fundamental questions about what children should learn, the best way to do this, what kinds of jobs they should be undertaking for the benefit of the economy, who should teach them (to name but a few educational debates) are issues of interest and concern not only to teachers, but also for others. These may include businesses who need a workforce; philosophers of education; those in authority (the government) who make decisions and invest public money in educational resources and services; and of course parents and carers. Therefore, it is an issue that many people are invested in both individually and collectively, and it demands a good deal of attention, enquiry and debate. By reading Education texts and resources with an enquiring mind, you will begin to become aware of a broad range of views, which will help to give you a more holistic, complete and balanced understanding of educational issues, and to understand that there are many different perspectives on almost every educational issue.

What to read?

There is an absolutely bewildering wealth of places where students can access information, and this can be very confusing and leave you feeling overwhelmed at where to begin when researching a topic. Traditionally, students needed to physically spend a lot of time in their university library, accessing books and journals (more explanation about journals to follow). Nowadays, many books and journals can be accessed online, as can a whole range of other sources. While this is advantageous to students who live away from campus or have other time-consuming responsibilities such as employment and families, having a greater number of places to search for material can also create pressure and feel like too much choice at times. The next section about the *different kinds* of sources available will help you to understand what are appropriate to use more or less of, and when.

There are many 'places' we can go to gather information on a subject, but not all of these are necessarily appropriate for use in academic work. The first thing to note here is that you may often hear people in the academic world (i.e. in universities) talking about '*academic* sources'. So, this begs the question, what makes a source 'academic'? This is our starting point here. As an example, let's consider how we would begin to find out information about university tuition fees, if this was an issue we needed to research (Activity 1.2).

ACTIVITY 1.2

Research sources

Can you identify five types of sources, or kinds of information you could access, to help you begin to research this subject?

1 _____

2 _____

3 _____

4 _____

5 _____

Your answers might have included:

- Government websites, for official policy and guidance about tuition fees (in the UK, the starting point would be www.gov.uk).
- Universities or colleges themselves – their websites, or face-to-face advice and information.
- Other websites relevant to students or prospective students (in the UK this might be the National Union of Students, for example).
- Academic textbooks that have scrutinised and discussed tuition fees, the reasons for them and their impact.
- Academic journal articles that have analysed various aspects of the tuition fee debate in detail or perhaps undertaken and written up research they have conducted – for example, gathering and analysing the views of prospective students and how they feel about paying tuition fees.
- Reports from other relevant organisations.
- Media reports or commentaries – for example, the BBC.
- A Google search.
- A library catalogue search.

All of the above can form suitable starting points when we need to undertake research on a subject. However, the extent to which we might actually use any of these sources can (and should) vary significantly, and there are several reasons for this. Firstly, unless you're instructed otherwise by your tutors, it's usually a good idea to try and inform yourself from a variety of different sources, so that you get used to routinely 'visiting' (either in person or virtually online) a number of different 'places' to access different kinds of information sources. Secondly, some careful thought is required about the nature of these kinds of sources, and it is important to realise that all of the sources listed above have very different purposes, and agendas. For example, a university website might point students to guidance about tuition fees with a generally positive and straightforward tone – after all, these institutions do not want students to see tuition fees as something problematic that might put them off studying. In contrast, a media report about tuition fees might be seeking to portray the views of a particular group of people, with a strongly worded or emotive headline in order to attract people to read their article (for reasons of finance and higher circulation figures).

It is crucial that you are aware of the varying motivations and purposes that may be behind a piece of writing, and that you do not simply accept what you read as the *only* point of view or a 'correct' piece of information. While it is true that in some instances, when you're searching for factual information such as the date of a piece of educational legislation, this is usually straightforward, remember that Education as an academic subject is grounded in a Social Sciences background, where there is generally no 'correct' answer or perspective to an issue – no 'right' or 'wrong' point of view, but simply many different and varied perspectives on any one issue. Your job as a student of Education is to show your awareness and understanding of some of these perspectives, and work towards making a well-informed judgement on that issue based on the evidence and information you have read.

What makes an information source 'academic'?

You may have noted in the list above that there are references to 'academic' books and journal articles. University lecturers will be used to frequently providing feedback to students along the lines of 'This is not a suitably academic source', but what does this actually mean? What is it that makes something 'academic'?

An academic source is a piece of work that has been produced by an individual(s) who is an expert in their area, and usually someone who is employed at a university or other kind of institution where a main component of their work is to advance or develop existing knowledge. This could be, for example, a medical researcher working in a laboratory researching treatments for a particular illness or condition. It might be a technical engineer working in the research and development section of a large industry where they are trying to produce new technologies. These will usually be individuals who have studied at university and higher levels (i.e. postgraduate degrees such as Master's or Doctoral studies; see Chapter 13) and advancing knowledge in their sector is an important part of their work.

In the area of Education, most of the 'producers' of academic sources of work will be those working in universities (or also further education colleges) as lecturers or tutors, or also you might come across those with the title of Reader or Professor, meaning that they have made significant contributions to knowledge in their area through their research. Collectively, these people are often referred to as 'academics', or they may describe their job role as being 'an academic'. Often, individuals in universities collaborate and work with other professionals in the areas they are researching, for example with school teachers or educational psychologists, meaning that the work produced is written by those who are particularly knowledgeable in their area; this is the first characteristic of 'academic' sources that distinguishes them from other types of information sources.

The second, and essential, characteristic of an 'academic' source compared to other kinds of information is related to what is known as 'peer review', which in its most basic sense means that the work produced by an individual (usually an academic in a university or similar institution) has been subject to scrutiny and review by others who are also experts in that field. This means that the quality of the work is assessed and evaluated in terms of its accuracy, the methods it may have used if data was gathered, and the relevance or importance of the issue. All of these areas will be commented upon by a number of experts, and the authors of the work will be required to make revisions and amendments based on the reviewers' recommendations before it can be approved for publication. This can be a very lengthy and time-consuming process, but it is an essential one whereby members of the academic community work together and support one another to, in effect, self-regulate and maintain standards of quality. The book you are reading now has been subject to peer review! Sources (or 'literature') that have been subjected to a peer review process are therefore perceived to be more reliable and credible than a general website or article you might find online, which may sound very well informed and convincing, but in reality could have been written by someone with very little expertise in their area.

A hierarchy of academic sources?

As mentioned earlier, it is good practice to become used to routinely accessing a range of sources when you are gathering information for your research and assignments. Envisioning a hierarchy or a ranking of sources can be helpful to identify which sources are preferential and which you should use more (or less) of (Figure 1.1).

The kinds of core sources (those you should use most often) that you will encounter in your studies then will be:

- Textbooks – designed for students studying a particular area, the chapters in a textbook have been carefully chosen by experts in that field to give you an insight into specific issues. Oftentimes textbooks are the best introductory source to begin researching a subject, as they can be quite general and trying to cover a wide range of issues. So, for example, textbooks that broadly cover 'Education Studies' will be ideal early on in your degree programme, but as you progress you will need to move on to more focused writing in order to understand issues at a greater depth.

Peer-reviewed academic journals

Academic books (e.g. textbooks)

Studies and research reports (e.g. from relevant organisations)

'Official' governmental publications or statistics

General websites (those you'd find from a Google search)

Generalised popular media

Anecdotal evidence (talking to friends, opinions of people)

Most desirable

Less desirable

Figure 1.1   A hierarchy of academic sources

- Monographs – these are more specialist books on a single subject, or aspect of it, usually written by just one individual who is particularly knowledgeable in that area.
- Policy documents – it's often necessary to refer to past or present policy documents, usually from government departments (such as the Department for Education) or other organisations. These are valuable to help us identify and then analyse the intentions behind government or local educational plans and practices. Always remember that the author(s) of a policy document will have some kind of agenda or an aim or outcome in mind.
- Journal articles – are much shorter than books, and written on very specific topics or issues. There exist an incredible amount of journal articles (sometimes also referred to as 'papers'). They are published throughout the year (whereas some information in a book might become outdated quite quickly) and tend to be written for a very academic audience.
- Relevant media sources – there are some publications (online, or in print form) that may be, in essence, newspapers or magazines, but are from a professional stance. For example, the *Times Educational Supplement*, or the *Times Higher Education Supplement*. These are publications written by journalists with a specialist interest in educational issues, writing for an educational audience, but remember they are still writing with a particular agenda or aiming to present an issue in a certain way.

ACTIVITY 1.3

Characteristics of different sources

Review the sources above, and with a peer or friend try to identify the pros and cons that may be associated with using each source. You should find a difference in the balance of these as you work your way down the list. See the answers at the end of the chapter.

Therefore, it should be apparent that not all sources are equal, and that being able to search through available literature effectively is a key skill for your Education degree.

Educational research

'Research' is the cornerstone of studies in Education. Academics and other relevant individuals (as mentioned earlier) work to produce vast amounts of research that analyses, evaluates and records experiences, perspectives, policies and strategies in the world of education. All of this information helps to better inform our thinking, planning and practice in areas of teaching, learning and training. A small insight into the amount and range of research studies being undertaken can be seen just by looking at the titles of articles featured in one educational academic journal in one month of the year, as presented in Box 1.1.

Box 1.1   The *British Educational Research Journal* (*BERJ*), Contents of Volume 43, Issue 4, August 2017:

The impact of Teach First on pupil attainment at age 16 (pages 627–646) Rebecca Allen and Jay Allnutt

Information and choice of A-level subjects: A cluster randomised controlled trial with linked administrative data (pages 647–670) Peter Davies, Neil M. Davies and Tian Qiu

Primary schools and network governance: A policy analysis of reception baseline assessment (pages 671–682) Guy Roberts-Holmes and Alice Bradbury

The consequences of being labelled 'looked-after': Exploring the educational experiences of looked-after children and young people in Wales (pages 683–699) Dawn Mannay, Rhiannon Evans, Eleanor Staples, Sophie Hallett, Louise Roberts, Alyson Rees and Darren Andrews

How do question writers compose external examination questions? Question writing as a socio-cognitive process (pages 700–719) Martin Johnson, Filio Constantinou and Victoria Crisp

Elite formation in the higher education systems of Ireland and the UK: Measuring, comparing and decomposing longitudinal patterns of cabinet members (pages 720–742) Sharon Feeney, John Hogan and Brendan K. O'Rourke

Multiple, relational and emotional mobilities: Understanding student mobilities in higher education as more than 'staying local' and 'going away' (pages 743–758) Kirsty Finn

The CANparent trial—the delivery of universal parenting education in England (pages 759–780) Stephen M. Cullen, Mairi-Ann Cullen and Geoff Lindsay

Modelling adult skills in OECD countries (pages 781–804) Rosario Scandurra and Jorge Calero

The development and validation of a scale measuring teacher autonomous behaviour (pages 805–821) Arnoud T. Evers, Peter Verboon and Andrea Klaeijsen

Source: http://onlinelibrary.wiley.com/doi/10.1111/berj.2017.43.issue-4/issuetoc 15 August 2017.

The wide range of journal articles (also sometimes referred to as 'papers' or 'studies') that can be seen from just one edition of one educational journal gives you a small insight into how much research is being published, and the kinds of very specific issues and areas that academics focus upon. The areas they have researched and written about may be due to personal interest, professional experience or a gap in the literature they feel needs filling (i.e. very little has been written about a particular issue or area). Often funding for particular studies (to pay for academics' time, resources and costs) may come from a particular organisation who needs to know more about a specific area, and so there may be a financial reason for the research to be undertaken.

Exploring journals

Using your university's online library portal, or main library web page, see if you can locate the Education journals and simply note the number of them and the kinds of different sectors or issues in the education system that they cover. If you're not sure how to do this, ask for help at the appropriate place in your library; you may be able to get some training or a demonstration of how to locate academic journals for your subject, and it's essential that you know how to locate these fairly early on in your degree programme.

Therefore, it is clear that a good deal of educational research is taking place and being published. However, 'research' can vary hugely, and sometimes the word is used in a misleading or inaccurate way. To pick up our example above about university tuition fees again, you could talk to ten people in your peer group about this issue and gather their overall impressions on the subject based upon their views: Is this research? In a way, it might be considered a kind of research, as it has been undertaken with a desire to better understand or discover something. However, it would not constitute research as we would understand in an academic sense, which is usually conducted in a systematic way, with clear objectives and specified methods of data collection that are thought to be reliable and effective. This is the difference between 'research' that might be conducted on an informal, personal basis and what we refer to as 'empirical' research, which is thorough enquiry into a particular area using specific techniques to collect data (e.g. interviews, questionnaires or statistical, numerical data) instead of opinion or belief. This is a good way to understand the difference between perspectives expressed in a media article versus perspectives presented in a peer-reviewed academic article.

Credibility and provenance of literature

'Credibility' and 'provenance' are two terms that are important to bear in mind when you are making decisions about what kinds of sources to use in your studies. This chapter has established so far that 'academic' sources should form the majority of your reading and research reflected in your assignments. However, there is a need to become even more discriminating about the sources you use, in order to help you narrow down your focus further and sift through the large number of sources you will find on any given topic.

Credibility depends on the extent to which we can place trust in an author or the literature they have published. This depends on the provenance of the source, which refers to the origins of something, or the ownership of something, which is a guide to its authenticity. In an academic sense, then, this means we need to consider and call into question where ideas and theories have come from and who is attributed to them. This will mean taking into account factors such as who the author is and what their position or potential bias might be.

Some institutions (e.g. the Open University, University of Bradford) suggest the use of the **PROMPT** (Presentation, Relevance, Objectivity, Method, Provenance, Timeliness) mnemonic to help you take a structured approach to evaluating a source:

Presentation – the impression created by the presentation of a source can make a big impact, and although it is not always the case that poor presentation equates to poor quality of content, observe how aspects of presentation might influence your ability to understand the points that the author is trying to make. This might include the language used, a confusing structure, and the general appearance and tidiness of the source.

Relevance – whether a source is relevant or not depends on what you have identified as your need. Take time before searching to make a list of key words or terms that reflect your specific subject or topic, to ensure you will get the most relevant results. This will also help you to be more efficient with your time, as often library searches on broad topics will return a staggering number of resources, and so narrowing these down with particular terms and using advanced search options will make the results more manageable for you.

Objectivity – the extent to which a source is objective or not may depend on the approach of the author(s) and their motivations for writing. There will be times when a piece of work is very explicit about the fact that they're presenting a case for or against an argument, or critiquing a theory, policy or another academic source. In such instances, the writing is unlikely to be entirely balanced, impartial and objective. Be observant too for research that may be sponsored (funded) by particular organisations or governmental departments, as this may impact upon what the researchers write, or how they interpret and present results. However, in most instances academic writing should represent a range of perspectives from an informed point of view.

Method – the nature of academic sources varies significantly. Some pieces of literature will be an analysis of an issue based on existing literature, and so this is referred to as use of secondary data. Primary data refers to information that has been gathered by a researcher in the form of interviews, questionnaires or other data collection methods (see Table 1.1 for a more detailed description of primary and secondary data source types). When primary data has been gathered, then some scrutiny should be paid to the approach and methods used, the sample used, the ethical considerations and the results. Useful texts to learn more about educational research in greater depth are listed at the end of this chapter.

Provenance – consider here the author(s) and be prepared to undertake a little research into them. Who is the individual(s) that has produced the source? What institution (e.g. university) are they based at? Is this an area that is a specialism for them? Has their work been cited (referred to) by lots of other authors? Has their research or report been sponsored (i.e. paid for) by a particular organisation, which might mean there is a potential bias in what they are reporting? Is it a source that we can expect to have been subject to peer review (i.e. usually a journal article)?

Timeliness – the date of publication may be significant to you; this depends on the nature of the source and the reason you need it. Sometimes you might need to access an original text written by an influential author from a hundred years ago. At other times you might need a particularly up-to-date perspective, or the most recent version of a document or set of statistics. Consider whether the date of publication meets your requirements and be sure you can find out when something has been published.

Table 1.1 Primary and Secondary data source types	
Primary data gathered by the researcher(s) for a specific purpose via ...	**Secondary data** already in existence and being utilised by a researcher or student for a specific purpose ...
Questionnaires/Surveys Interviews Focus groups Visual data such as photographs or drawings Observations (notes and records taken) Journals/diaries Experiments	Reports Journal articles Books Existing images/photographs Statistics (e.g. published by a government department) Websites Government legislation (Acts of Parliament) Media reports*

*remember the hierarchy of sources pyramid in Figure 1.1

Chapter summary: useful points for you to implement

- Reading a *range* of sources will form an important component of your studies as an Education student. Of particular importance is the need to gain breadth and depth; to identify where ideas have come from when you refer to them; and to gain an understanding of different perspectives on an issue.
- A range of different sources need to be drawn upon, but those from the upper ends of the hierarchy (books and journals) are usually preferable, and you should look to include work that has been peer-reviewed in your reading and assignments.
- Empirical research that represents thorough and systematic enquiry is more reliable than representations of opinions or beliefs and should form a substantial part of the sources you draw upon.
- Use the PROMPT mnemonic to help you assess the credibility and provenance of information sources before committing to using them.

Answers to Activity 1.3

Some of the pros and cons associated with these kinds of sources include:

Source	Pros	Cons
Peer-reviewed journal article	Up-to-date Specialised Peer-reviewed	Can be written in very technical language The vast number means searching needs to be very strategic
Academic books	Written by specialist authors Peer-reviewed Brings together a lot of knowledge on one issues into one place	Some parts may be out of date within a few years An author may have one particular viewpoint which may not be representative of all perspectives
Studies and research reports	Often well-funded and may be able to present extensive research on an issue	Usually published by particular organisations with a certain agenda
Government statistics or publications	Access to up-to-date statistical information is an essential context for our discussions	Criteria and methods used to gather statistics may not always be transparent
General websites	Often explain issues in an easy to understand manner – can be a great starting point to research an issue	The provenance of the information presented cannot be verified
Generalised popular media	Can be a useful indicator of certain views on a subject	May be written from a particularly left or right wing perspective, or seeking to be sensationalist in order to attract readers
Anecdotal evidence	Individuals' experiences or viewpoints are valid insights and can be a useful way to gain an insight into an issue	Evidence based on just one person's experience or point of view cannot be relied upon to give a balanced or all-round picture on an issue

How Should I Be Reading?

The previous chapter established that *what* you read should be your primary consideration, and this chapter supplies you with more detailed and specific strategies so that once you have located the sources you're going to use, you can use them most effectively.

In this chapter we will cover:

- How to search sources effectively to find the most relevant information for your tasks and study.
- Different approaches to reading to help you make the most of your time.
- Developing your reading skills to become more reflective.

Searching effectively

Your starting point to help you read the most *relevant* materials will be your course or module's reading list, tutor recommendations or tasks, and also the learning outcomes or overall aims of the module or course you're studying. These are all initial steps that can help you to narrow your focus. If in doubt, ask your tutors, especially if you are considering spending money on particular books, as they can be expensive (although used/second-hand books can be suitable, especially if they don't need to be the most up-to-date edition).

The next step in ensuring your reading is purposeful and effective is to work further on ensuring the sources you draw upon are *directly relevant* for your purposes. Oftentimes you will be using search engines of some sort to help you narrow down results. These search engines might be:

- A library catalogue that searches through all the contents your library can give you access to – for example, books on the shelves; e-books; journals; e-journals; reports; newspaper; or image archives.
- A general search engine such as Google or Google Scholar (these are acceptable places to start your research before you narrow down to use more academic sources).
- Academic Databases via your library website to help you find specific journal articles that may be on a reading list, or to search using terms to find journal articles about specific subjects or issues.

ACTIVITY 2.1

Refining search terms

You have been asked to research the history of **independent schools** for some group work. Can you think of five key words you might use as search terms to start finding information?

1 _____

2 _____

3 _____

4 _____

5 _____

Some of your answers might have included:

- Private or elite schools
- Public schools (the American terminology)
- Educational privilege
- Eton/Rugby (i.e. famous independent schools)
- Independent schools, charities
- Private schools, scholarships

As you can imagine, typing each of these terms into a search engine is going to bring up very different results compared to just searching with the term 'history of independent schools'. So, searching very often begins with broad terms, then as you come across a range of issues, ideas and perspectives on that issue, you can draw up a list of more specific terms to use; this is how you can narrow down search results from thousands to a more manageable number that you can begin to work with.

Within your university's search engine, or those within an academic database, you are usually given the options to further narrow down your search (e.g. using an Advanced Search option) according to:

- Date range (by typing dates into a box or selecting on a sliding scale – for example, selecting dates within a certain range, such as from 2010 to the present day).
- Language – selecting only those articles published in English.
- Whether they are peer-reviewed or not (sometimes referred to as 'scholarly').
- Publication type – that is, journal/newspaper/book/report.

You are also given the options to combine search words or author names (using 'AND'), with the possibility of narrowing down further to search for the words in the publication's title, subject terms, all of the text, or the abstract (see the following section). There are a number of specialist databases for the subject of Education, such as Education Database, British Education Index or Education Resources Information Center (ERIC). Google, or Google Scholar, are less well-suited to academic research as they do not allow you to use as many criteria to narrow down your search. They are also less likely to produce results that would pass the PROMPT provenance criteria discussed in the previous chapter.

Most university or college libraries have specialist librarians or staff who can assist you with searches or your institution may provide training sessions to help you learn how to use various search mechanisms for information seeking – it is well worth your time attending these.

Abstracts

An 'abstract' is a brief summary of the content of a publication (most often a journal article) which you can read quite quickly to help you decide whether the content is relevant to you, similar to the information (or 'blurb') on the back of a book. An abstract will usually include some rationale for the issue being discussed, that is, a 'problem' or discussion that is being examined; the approach used by the author(s), that is, whether the publication is a piece of primary research or a review of existing literature; the results or key findings; and the conclusions.

ACTIVITY 2.2

Reading an abstract

Reading the abstract below, can you identify:

1 The focus of the article? (in your own words)

2 What the primary research entailed? (i.e. what the researchers actually did)

3 What the findings of the research were?

This paper explores hidden messages sent out by schools about Oxbridge, using Basil Bernstein's concepts of classification and framing. Research in three case-study schools captured these messages from their everyday practices and processes, including their events and activities, sorting mechanisms, interactions and resources. Whilst all of the schools sent out strong classificatory messages, marking out Oxbridge as special, they differed in their strength of framing, making explicit to differing degrees which students are 'Oxbridge material'.

Source: Donnelly, M. (2014) 'The road to Oxbridge: schools and elite university choices', *British Journal of Educational Studies*, Vol. 62, No. 1, pp. 57–72.

Approaches to reading

As stressed in Chapter 1, the amount of reading required for an Education degree should not be underestimated! Therefore, it is essential that you develop some strategies to make the most of your time and read effectively.

Did you know that there are different kinds of reading required for academic study? It is helpful to learn to use a mixture of these different approaches, as each serves a different purpose. Below is an outline of four approaches that you will find helpful:

● **Skimming** – this means reading quickly to identify broad, overall ideas in a piece of text (to get the 'gist' of it). For some people, this means that they don't actually need to read every word, but can just identify and pick out key words to get an understanding of the ideas being presented.

- **Scanning** – this requires looking over a piece of writing rapidly, trying to pick out specific information – for example, particular words or terms, or perhaps some statistics.
- **Active or purposeful reading** – this usually means that you are reading for a specific purpose, often to be able to select points from that reading to answer a question.
- **Critical reading** – think back to the PROMPT mnemonic in Chapter 1; this is a good starting point to consider the nature and characteristics of what you are reading. Think about who the author is and their provenance; do they support their claims with evidence; is it an opinion piece or based on empirical evidence; how have they come to their conclusions; are other perspectives represented; and what methods were used for primary data collection?

ACTIVITY 2.3

Implementing different approaches to reading a piece of text

Read the passage below and then try to answer the subsequent questions. If you come across words that you do not know the meaning of, check in a dictionary and write a definition in your own words.

Bates et al. (2011) define education policy as 'The raft of laws and initiatives that determine the shape and functioning of educational systems at both national and local level' (p. 54). As education is so important in any society, it will form a major part of any government's plans. If we accept the premise above that educational aims have an ideological basis, then education policy is the plan or blueprint by which these aims are put into practice. It is likely that due to changes in social and economic circumstances these policies will be amended and adapted. For instance, introducing school or university reform during times of economic restraint can significantly affect what any government is able to do. It is also likely that policy will be challenged by those with opposing ideologies. A change of government is likely to lead to an ideological shift, thus aspects of the education system are in a continual state of being 'reformed'. Successive governments, for instance, have altered the content and assessment of the school curriculum and also the structure of secondary schooling. Of course politicians also have to respond to external events and so changes introduced may be reactive rather than proactive, for example corporal punishment was finally abolished in schools due to a European ruling on human rights rather than the beliefs of the sitting Conservative English government.

As the importance of formal education has grown significantly over the last 200 years, so has the role of the state – and in turn the government that happens to be in power – in shaping educational developments. The study of education policy to a very large extent involves examining the intent and actions of governments, their ability to implement their particular policies and the effects of that implementation. As each new government assumes that its approach to education will change things for the better all policy changes are presented as 'reforms'.

Source: Bartlett, S. and Burton, D. (2012) *Introduction to Education Studies*. London: SAGE Publications, p. 134.

Questions

1 *Active* reading question: What is one of the influences upon education policy change mentioned in this except?

2 *Critical* reading question: How credible and reliable do you think this piece of writing is? Can you find out about the authors and their credentials? Does the passage come across as objective? Is the date of publication significant?

3 *Skimming* reading question: What is the key message or idea within this passage?

4 *Scanning* reading question: Which policy does the piece refer to that was abolished due to Human Rights law?

See the end of the chapter for answers.

It can be seen from this exercise that reading for different purposes requires different levels of attention, a different focus, more or less time, and also perhaps further research (e.g. to find out about the provenance of the authors). Therefore, a key point to take away here to make your reading more efficient is to ensure you are aware of what the *purpose* of your reading is. Do you simply need a few small pieces of information, facts or statistics? Do you need to be able to feed back to your tutor what the overall idea was? Or, do you need to be able to reflect a deeper understanding and answer specific questions about the ideas, theories and reasoning presented in the text? The latter requires more time than the former; so always try to make sure you are reading with a purpose, and that you know what that purpose is.

Approaching large chunks of reading

The passage above about education policy is a small piece of writing; you will be required to read much longer and more complex texts as you progress throughout your studies. This can be daunting and also require a lot of your time. However, remember *you are reading for a degree*!

TIP

Time spent reading is one of the best investments students can make in their learning at degree level, not only so that you can answer questions such as those above, but crucially so that you can expose yourself to a wide range of different perspectives, ideas, opinions, research findings and experiences that you can then use to develop your own understanding, and reflect this in your assignments.

When you have large amounts of reading to do, here are a few considerations that may help you to approach such a task:

1 Think about what is *essential* and what is supplementary or recommended. Always prioritise the essential reading because tutors have classified it as essential for a reason.
2 Consider the purpose of the reading (as discussed above).
3 How much time do you have? When are you going to be able to undertake the reading? Is the time available to you in short bursts, or is it long and sustained? How much time do you need to allow to work your way through the reading required? For most people, very focused reading that requires a lot of concentration is difficult to sustain for more than 20–30 minutes, and so learn to recognise when you are reading the same sentence repeatedly, and take a short break or vary your study activity.
4 What is the best kind of environment and circumstances for you to be able to read? Think about your posture, noise and lighting – all of these things can affect your ability to read well. If you are reading electronic materials on a computer or tablet, turn off notifications and sounds. Move your phone away from you so it is out of reach and sight, and turn it to silent.
5 How will you retain or use the information from your reading? Do you need to take notes? If so, this will take further time – (see Chapter 3) for more guidance on taking notes and making notes.
6 Consider studying together with someone else on your course, and discuss your understanding of a piece of reading if you have the opportunity to do so; note how you will both have taken away different key messages or interpreted the same points or passages differently.

Reading large chunks of text effectively

The steps below can be useful to follow so that you have a strategy and purpose for reading when trying to work your way through longer pieces of text, such as a book chapter or journal article:

1 Skim the text to get an overall idea of key content, ideas and conclusions. Check that this is relevant and fits your needs – remember to ask what the purpose of your reading is? Use an abstract, contents page or searches for key words in a piece of text to make sure you're certain that it is relevant to you.
2 Settle down and read the content thoroughly, without rushing.
3 While you are reading, highlight passages you feel are particularly relevant, check the definitions of words you don't understand, and indicate to yourself (perhaps with the use of a question mark) if there are any parts you don't understand that you might need help with (e.g. asking a tutor or reading about the same point in a different text).
4 It can be useful to write (in your own words) a summary of the text, a few key points that reflect the overall ideas, findings or perspective in the work. Also, note down if you disagree with any points made, or if you have any uncertainty or scepticism about anything the authors are saying, especially with regard to the

kinds of evidence the authors provide to support their claims, or the methods they might have used to gather any primary data, and how they might have interrupted this.

5 Make sure you record the details of what you have read (i.e. the author(s), date of publication, title and publication details or web address). This is important so that you can reference it correctly, and find it again if you need to reread it.

Below is an example of the same passage about education policy, annotated to illustrate some of the points above that can make your reading a more effective and engaging experience for you:

Bates et al. (2011) define education policy as "The raft of <u>laws and initiatives that determine the shape and functioning of educational systems</u> at both national and local level" (p.54). As education is so important in any society, it wilt form a major part of any government's plans. If we accept the premise above that <u>educational aims have an ideological basis</u>, then <u>education policy is the plan or blueprint</u> by which these aims are put into practice. It is likely that due to changes in social and economic circumstances these policies will be amended and adapted. For instance, introducing school or university reform *→ change* during times of economic restraint can significantly affect what any government is able to do. It is also likely that policy will be challenged by those with opposing ideologies. <u>A change of government is likely to lead to an ideological shift</u>, thus aspects of the education system are in a <u>continual state of being 'reformed'</u>. Successive governments, for instance, have altered the content and assessment of the school curriculum and also the structure of secondary schooling. Of course politicians also have to respond to <u>external events</u> and so changes introduced may be reactive rather than proactive, for example corporal punishment was finally abolished in schools due to a European ruling on human rights rather than the beliefs of the sitting Conservative English government.

ideals or beliefs, usually political

→ effects of budget

i.e. different political party

look for more examples

increasing provision and intervention

As the importance of formal education has grown significantly over the last 200 years, <u>so has the role of the state</u> – and in turn the government that happens to be in power – in shaping educational developments. The study of education policy to a very large extent involves <u>examining the intent and actions of governments, their ability to implement their particular policies and the effects of that implementation</u>. As each new government assumes that its approach to education will change things for the better <u>all policy changes are presented as 'reforms'</u>. *positive spin?*

①intentions
②implementation
③consequences

Bartlett, S. and Burton, D. (2012) *Introduction to Education Studies* *London*: SAGE Publications Ltd

Reading reflectively

As you progress in your studies, you will need to read more *reflectively* in order to demonstrate more independent and critical thinking about what you have read. Doing so requires you to engage with the text and ask questions about *what* you are reading, and indeed ask questions about your own thoughts *as* you are reading. In addition to just repeating or re-presenting what you have learned from a text, you will need to integrate ideas from several sources, think about them and present your own individual, balanced point of view based on what you have read.

The earlier exercise about approaches to reading education policy illustrated that there can be different kinds of reading. A next step is to not just accept what you read and use it in isolation, but to extend your understanding and enquiry by taking what you have learnt from your reading a step further.

Reading reflectively does not necessarily mean *criticising* what you read; it means thinking beyond what is presented to you in that one piece of reading and making connections to other perspectives, ideas and knowledge that you may have gathered through various sources, such as lecture notes or the views of your fellow students.

Here are some prompts to help you think about what you are reading in a more reflective manner:

1 What does this add to what you already know about the issue or subject? Is it reiterating the same ideas and perspectives or presenting new ones?
2 Are there more up-to-date perspectives or policy changes since this source was published?
3 When exploring policies or strategies, consider why they might have been developed and implemented, and subsequently what was the impact of them? Look for sources that have written around or *about* particular policies (i.e. commentary on them or evaluations) rather than just the policy or strategy itself.
4 Do you think there are key things that have been left out by this particular piece of writing?

A final note about reading ...

Reading at degree level can seem overwhelming, and it is important to stress that everyone has different reading abilities and speeds. Some people are able to skim very quickly, but need to spend a good deal of time rereading a source to fully understand it. Some people love reading and revel in it, while for others it is really challenging. Becoming familiar with some of the strategies outlined in this chapter, and working to implement them, will help you to use your time more efficiently, and to achieve more awareness and understanding in your studies.

If you have a specific learning difficulty (such as dyslexia) then you may understandably feel particularly anxious about reading for your degree. While everyone who has dyslexia experiences it differently, be aware that the amount of time you need to read may be increased, and that you might need to implement specific strategies to help you organise and recall what you come across in your reading. Be sure to make use of your institution's support services for students with specific learning difficulties (such as support workers to help you plan and proofread). If you have never had an assessment for a specific learning difficulty but feel concerned that you may have difficulties, go to your institution's disability support services for some initial advice; they may recommend an assessment for you.

Some useful resources:

- Dyslexia Action: www.dyslexiaaction.org.uk
- British Dyslexia Association: www.bdadyslexia.org.uk

Chapter summary: useful points for you to implement

- Take time to develop your searching skills and use the support on offer from your institution to do this.
- Practice effective reading strategies such as skimming to decide whether it is worth your while reading whole articles or chapters.
- Read purposefully and reflectively to develop your viewpoint on ideas and perspectives you come across.

Answers to Activity 2.3

1 You could have identified social, economic, political ideologies, change in government, external events.
2 The authors Bartlett and Burton (Steve Bartlett and Diana Burton) are both Professors of Education and the book from which this excerpt was taken has been published many times with a number of different editions (i.e. more up-to-date versions). It is one of the most commonly recommended textbooks for students of Education in the early years of their degree programmes. Although the excerpt here is from their 2012 edition, the basic premise of the points they are conveying is not dependent upon dates. While a more recently written piece could refer to more up-to-date examples of policy, the overall message remains the same. Their writing is not seeking to be particularly persuasive, controversial or biased towards one political idea or another; it is intended to be an objective appraisal of the nature of education policy in this country and some of its characteristics.
3 The key message of this piece is that education policy is crucial in society, but that it can be subject to many factors and changes frequently depending upon the government tin power and their ideas.
4 The policy of corporal punishment (i.e. physically punishing pupils, such as with a cane) was abolished due to Human Rights law.

Taking Notes and Making Notes

Whether it's with a notepad and pen, or on a tablet or laptop, you will need to spend time taking notes in lectures, seminars, workshops and also from various sources that you read. Most of this chapter is focused upon traditional notes (i.e. writing text) but also bear in mind that other approaches to condensing information such as drawing mind maps, diagrams or tables, or even recording your own voice (e.g. using a voice memo/recorder facility on your phone or computer) can be good strategies.

In this chapter you will learn:

- The difference between note taking and note making, and which to use when.
- Practical techniques for recording notes, organising and reviewing them.

Note taking and note making: what's the difference?

Note *taking* is usually what you would be expected to do in a lecture, or other scenario where information is being delivered to you. It can also go hand in hand with active reading (as outlined in the previous chapter). It is a more passive approach, whereby you are more or less recording (by writing down with pen, paper or on laptop or tablet) what is being said, or read. The purpose of note taking is to have a *record* of what has been said, or presented to you.

Note *making* is a slightly more advanced approach where you are writing out your own understanding of a topic, issue, theory, event or strategy as a result of ideas from one or more sources that you have reflected upon and are synthesising in your own words. The purpose of note *making* is to develop your own understanding and recording it in a way that makes sense to you.

Consider the aims of your note making:

- For your own revision or understanding?
- To pass on to someone else?
- To identify useful points/evidence/information to include in an assignment?
- To understand a substantial chapter or article in depth?

These differing purposes will help to guide you as to what kind of notes you should take or make.

Techniques for taking notes

Oftentimes, taking notes can be a rushed event (e.g. trying to record a lot of information in a lecture or similar setting) and so it might seem odd to try to think about implementing a technique here. However, adopting a thought-out approach can make a positive impact upon the quality of your notes, which ultimately form a valuable learning resource. In this section, firstly some approaches that can be used 'live' in a lecture setting are outlined. Secondly, if taking a particular approach to taking notes in a lecture setting doesn't work for you, then you need to consider what you are going to do with those notes *after* the lecture.

Taking notes in a 'live' setting

It can be challenging to take notes in a 'live' setting such as a lecture or presentation where someone is delivering a stream of information to you that can sometimes feel quite fast. Think about the following to consider what the best approach might be for you:

- **Advance notes:** Find out if some kind of outline or notes for that lecture or session are available *prior* to the class. Some institutions and their tutors make materials available to students before scheduled classes through their Virtual Learning Environment (VLE) such as Blackboard or Moodle. This might mean you are able to download (and/or print out) the session's key points in advance, and then write your own notes around them, thus saving you time, and giving you a structure to work to.
- **Try audio:** In some circumstances, you may be given permission to make audio recordings of material being presented to you – this is quite a common occurrence for students with a recognised specific learning difficulty, who may be supplied with recording equipment by their institution. *Always* check that this is acceptable to the person who is delivering a lecture to you, and be aware that on occasions where other students contribute to discussions, they may not want their opinions and viewpoints recorded.
- **Condense the message:** Don't write down precisely what is said word for word – unless you are an exceptionally fast typist or are lucky enough to know shorthand; accept that it is impossible to record every word, and nor is this desirable: no lecturer or presenter wants to face a room full of people with their heads bowed taking notes. Those teaching you want to see and make eye contact with people that are clearly listening and engaged, so that they can receive some feedback about what is being heard and understood.
- **Take shortened notes:** Abbreviate, use symbols and perhaps take pictures of slides/diagrams or what might be written on a whiteboard (check it is okay with the tutor or presenter to do this). As long as *you* understand what you have written, do it in your own style … just make sure it is legible.
- **Highlight quotes:** When you write down word for word what has been said, or record material that has been presented to you on a slide or board, indicate this with the use of quotation marks ('xxxx') so that you know these are someone else's words that you cannot write out in an assessed piece of work without acknowledging their source.

- **Colour code:** If you can juggle a variety of stationery, have different coloured pens to hand and develop your own code or key as to what each colour indicates – for example, highlighting very important points in yellow, key dates in green and so on.
- **Be organised:** Start every new session or lecture by clearly indicating (to yourself) the date, module or course, subject and tutor on your new document. You might wish to be even more organised and prepare a template to record notes depending on your preference, as illustrated in Figure 3.1.

When taking notes from a source such as a book, journal article, report or website, be sure to record the following details:

- Author (s): write their names out, bearing in mind the author may be more than one person, an organisation or a government department. It is usual in most referencing conventions to record a person's surname and initial for example, Smith, J. (see Chapter 4 for further points about referencing).
- The date: in a book this is usually found within the first few pages with the publication details. For journal articles it is always apparent on the first page or in a header or footer. On reports, it should be near the front, or on the back page. On web pages, if there is no obvious publication date for a source, look for any indication of when the page was 'last updated'. If there is no publication date on a website, then you should go back to some of the points in Chapter 1 and ask

Module: Educational Theories 100 Date: April 10th	Tutor: John Smith Topic: Behaviourist approaches
Overall aims/learning outcomes:	
Lecture notes:	**Key points/terms/references**
Questions/follow up/key reading:	

Figure 3.1   Suggested template for note taking

yourself if this casts aspersions on the provenance or credibility of the source? Alternatively, 'no date' can be recorded but it is always preferable to be able to record a date of publication.

- The full title of the book/chapter/article and the full web link if it is an online source.
- Publication details such as the name of the publishers (again, found within the first few pages of a book), or the full title of a journal. Journals also have additional identifying information such as their volume and issue numbers, and the page range of the particular article, so write all of this down.
- Again, **always indicate when you are copying word for word by using quotation marks, so that you do not mistake someone else's words for your own** and potentially plagiarise work.

Get into the habit of recording these details before taking notes from any source, and this will make your referencing easier, and ensure you always know where your ideas have come from.

Your 'notes' might not always be written: taking pictures, using audio recordings or making mind maps of information from sources are also good ways to record things, as long as you have systems to record where they have come from. If you're not keen on writing and prefer to record and view things visually, then you may wish to take notes from sources via a mind map, as illustrated in Figure 3.2.

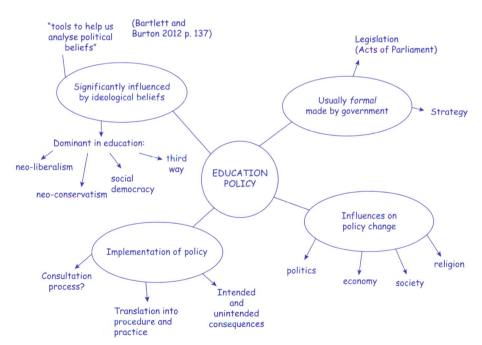

Figure 3.2   Example of a mind map

Organising and reviewing notes

However you take and record notes, remember it is crucial to organise them, record where you have taken your information from accurately, and make sure you go back to revisit them to help your understanding. You will be grateful for your efforts when you return to your notes for an assignment or exam.

If you work on a tablet or laptop, you could create a folder for each lecture, and then use this to store your own notes, materials supplied by the tutor before and afterwards, pictures or audio recordings (if permitted) and links to, or copies of, relevant reading. If you prefer to have things in hard copy (on paper), then invest in some files and store and organise your notes in a logical manner – for example, one folder per module or course – using dividers for each subject or lesson.

Remember that there will always come a point when you need to revisit and review the notes you have made, and so being able to locate them will be important. Good practice to help you recall and understand content as you go along in your studies would be to take notes from a class, revisit them shortly afterwards (before you forget!) to make additions or amendments, supplement them with ideas from additional reading and then perhaps *make* a new set of notes based on your own understanding. If you file your notes away at the end of a class and then don't look at them again until an assessment is due a few months later, you might have to undertake a lot more work to remember and reacquaint yourself with that topic.

Chapter summary: useful points for you to implement

- Always try to be aware of what the *purpose* of your note-taking is, so that you can approach it with the most appropriate strategies and amount of time available.
- Annotate and make notes so that they make sense to *you*.
- Take time to organise your notes carefully, and be sure to meticulously record where you are taking your information from.

Referencing and Avoiding Plagiarism

Drawing on literature in your assessed work demonstrates wider reading around a topic and can illustrate your knowledge and understanding. It can also be used as evidence for your viewpoint to help you to support the arguments you're making in your work. Alongside this comes referencing, which is a central aspect of academic writing. Clearly written and accurate referencing means that there is a trail of information about the different sources of information used within a piece of writing. It means that other readers who are interested in finding out about the original source can easily find it. Referencing the work of others also ensures good practice and academic integrity so that you are not plagiarising other's work.

This chapter goes into greater depth about the mechanics of referencing and:

- Explains the reasons for using academic references in your work.
- Illustrates ways in which you might typically do this, with examples of quotations and paraphrasing.
- Advises you on approaches required to avoid plagiarising.

Referencing and acknowledging sources in your work

Referencing is an academic skill whereby we document and record the various sources used to inform and contribute to a piece of work. You will have seen in the earlier excerpt about education policy (Chapter 2) that the authors refer to the surnames and dates of other writers' work; this is referred to as *in-text referencing* or a *citation* and acknowledges the source of an idea or piece of information or identifies where a quotation has been taken from. It is then academic convention (and a requirement) to document all the sources you refer to in a list at the end of the publication, or assignment, to create a Reference List. Therefore, you must keep careful records of which information sources (books, journal articles, reports, legislation, websites) you have used in order to reference them correctly, by taking down the details of each source as outlined in the previous section on taking notes.

Every institution has its own guidance on how to reference, and there will usually be sessions either at the level of your course, or more centrally, to help you to learn how to reference correctly. When you take the time to learn how to reference early on in your studies, so that this becomes part of your habits and good academic practice, this also means that you are not at risk of either losing marks on your work or unintentionally plagiarising.

Ensuring you acknowledge sources and/or paraphrase the work of others into your own words will help you to promote your own 'writing voice' and the overall academic tone of the piece of work as well as avoid plagiarism. Because Education subjects are located within the Social Sciences and much academic writing is based on researching people, this means that gathering their thoughts and perceptions and then analysing and interpreting them is the norm, rather than dealing in indisputable facts. Although many students are hesitant to question the work of 'expert' academics and researchers and to state their own arguments, you should be more confident in your own ideas, and acknowledging sources/rephrasing the work of others will help you to do this.

There are a number of different systems (or methods) of referencing, each of which has particular rules and conventions. In Education, the most common form of referencing is referred to as the Harvard system or method. It is very important to use your own institution and course documentation and guidance about how to reference, as even within the Harvard system of referencing, there can be small variations. For the purposes of your assessed work, you should always follow the specific guidance you have been given, which is why there is not a comprehensive guide to referencing supplied in this book.

Quoting and paraphrasing

Broadly, references in assignments can take two forms:

1 Paraphrasing: where you refer to an idea you've taken from a source, and then cite the author's name and date of their work.
2 The inclusion of a direct quotation, where you reproduce someone else's words precisely, and acknowledge this.

Paraphrasing the work of others

One way of using the work of others is to acknowledge the author or source, summarise it and rephrase their ideas in your own words. The process of summarising and paraphrasing the writing will demonstrate to your lecturer your ability to read, synthesise, summarise and use sources to develop your arguments. Reading a text critically and more than once to make sure you have understood the ideas and arguments (see Chapter 1) is a must. While reading you should make notes, summarising the key points and arguments in your own writing. Avoid copying down exactly the same words when writing your summary because it's important to keep the ideas that you're reading about and your summary and your own thoughts and ideas separate. You should then read your summary critically to check that you have still presented the key original ideas through using your words to explain them now. In the examples below you can see the difference between a direct quotation and paraphrasing.

So, *a paraphrase is your own interpretation and expression of ideas expressed by someone else*. In order to do this, read the passage or phrases carefully, ensure you understand the main idea and then think about how you would express this in your own words (although beware of sounding too conversational).

Paraphrasing example

The original text found here is as follows:

> The introduction of alternative provision in 1994 was in response to national concerns regarding the social and educational outcomes of students excluded from mainstream school, due to challenging behaviour. Specifically, Pupil Referral Units (PRUs) are the most frequent form of alternative provision. (Jalali and Morgan, 2018, p. 55)

An example of this paraphrased could be:

> The most common type of alternative provision for pupils excluded from mainstream schools for behavioural reasons is Pupil Referral Units (PRUs), introduced in 1994 as a result of concerns about the consequences of exclusion (Jalali and Morgan, 2018).

NOTE: You must still include the reference to acknowledge where you have taken the idea, or information from, but there's no need for a page number because it's not a direct quotation.

Directly quoting others' work

When you begin your academic writing journey, and/or when you come across unfamiliar ideas or perhaps more complex theories that are difficult to understand, you may feel more inclined to directly quote (i.e. reproduce word for word) a passage of text. Students say that doing this feels safer because they're not fully sure of their understanding. However, quotations alone do not help you to demonstrate knowledge and understanding of topics, theories and concepts, so you shouldn't rely on them in your writing. Instead, good reasons for using quotations can be that:

- You can use them to support viewpoints and build arguments being made.
- You may feel that the writer expresses the point in such a relevant and well-expressed way that you want to convey this exactly.
- It might be important or relevant to your work to cite someone's words precisely to ensure they are accurately represented.

Try to go for a balance of both quotations and paraphrases in your work. As you move into the second and third years of your degree programme, try to rely less on quotations (especially lengthy ones) and use more paraphrasing, which is better for showing your understanding to those reading (and assessing) your work. So, be careful to not overuse direct quotations; remember that they are the words and writing of other authors that you have borrowed and including such quotations may disrupt the flow of your own voice in your writing. Although quotations can illustrate to a lecturer that you can copy text accurately, on their own they do not demonstrate your ability to construct an argument, or convey your understanding.

When including a direct quotation:

- Use text to embed and introduce it
- Be sure to use quotation marks
- Copy the quotation exactly
- Include the details of the author(s), date of publication and page number

- Be aware that usual practice requires quotations of approximately three lines or longer to be indented within the paragraph.

As always, check with your lecturers about specific guidelines and practices for your course.

> **TIP**
>
> **Presenting references at the end of the work**
>
> When coming to collate and present all your references at the end, note that some assignments might require you to submit a Bibliography, but that this differs from a Reference list. A Reference list should only feature sources you have used (mentioned) in your assignment. A Bibliography is a reflection of everything you have *read* or consulted, to inform yourself for that assignment. Most pieces of assessed work will insist on just a Reference list, but again, this is a detail that you should clarify with your tutor(s).

Understanding plagiarism

Plagiarism in its most basic form is passing off someone else's words or ideas as your own, whether intentional or not. This is a concern in academia not just because it constitutes a form of cheating (or 'unfair means'), but because it is part of a much wider principle known as 'academic integrity', which is underpinned by values such as honesty, moral behaviour, maintaining high standards and respecting the work of those who generate new knowledge in their field. When you become a student, you become a member of an academic community whereby teachers, researchers and learners are all joined in their shared pursuit of a greater understanding, and so there is an expectation that all the members of this community will abide by the rules associated with academic integrity. Each university has its own definition of plagiarism that you will be able to find in their academic regulations, but it is more complex than just copying someone else's words in an assignment. Another relevant term used that you may come across is *collusion*, whereby an individual works together with another person(s) to submit work that is assessed individually, and therefore what has been submitted has been falsely presented as the work of one individual.

When considering how to describe plagiarism, the University of East Anglia's policy (UEA, 2017a) on Plagiarism and Collusion describes the concept and we couldn't think of a more appropriate phrasing which is that: *'Plagiarism is presenting someone else's work (words or ideas) as your own, i.e. without acknowledgement.'*

Plagiarism, or some kind of 'cheating', can occur either intentionally or unintentionally as a result of:

- Copying down someone else's words, ideas, experiences or opinions without acknowledging the source (i.e. without providing a reference). Even if you write things out in your own words (referred to as 'paraphrasing'), you must still include a reference to make it clear where you have taken the idea or point of view from.
- Purchasing or taking an essay written by someone else via a website or from a fellow student.

- Working too closely with another student when the work should be your own; while it is effective and productive to share resources and discuss your understanding of issues covered on your degree programme, unless work is of a group nature (e.g. a project or presentation) then what you present for assessment should be your own. Therefore, in most instances it is not in your interests to share your work with other students, as even if you trust them completely, you could still find yourself in trouble for doing this.
- Using work you have done previously for other courses or modules. Even if you change sections of it, you can plagiarise your own work, and this is poor academic practice because, essentially, you are not undertaking the required amount of work for each assignment. Therefore, copying and pasting paragraphs or sections from other assignments into a new piece of work is not acceptable. If you are uncertain about the kinds of ideas, references or material you can or cannot use from previous studies, always ask your tutors.

Apart from the fact that institutions can implement quite harsh penalties for plagiarism (e.g. failing a piece of work or a module in its entirety), referencing correctly and acknowledging the source of your ideas is an important part of academic integrity and respect for those who have worked to advance our understanding in an area.

TIP

Avoiding plagiarism

Key ways to avoid plagiarising are to produce individual work on your own, and to keep careful records of where you have taken your ideas from.

Most institutions also require some, or all assessed work to be submitted online via software that checks students' work for signs of plagiarism, by scanning and comparing what you have written with already published work, and other students' assignments at your own and other institutions – for example, software such as Turnitin or Copycatch. Some institutions may make this facility available to students to enable you to review your own work prior to a final submission. If you have the opportunity to do this, make sure you do so, as this is a useful tool to allow you to double-check how meticulous you have been with your referencing.

Chapter summary: useful points for you to implement

- Remember to make a note of all the bibliographic/referencing information as you go along rather than having to find details at the end.
- Do not attempt to copy others' work (writing, ideas and arguments) or resubmit your work twice for different assessments – it's plagiarism.
- Find out about your own institution's referencing guidance, workshops or support for this, and the kinds of plagiarism software that might be available to you to help you check your own work.

Thinking Critically for an Education Degree

Critical thinking is a term thrown around a great deal in university courses, and it can be a source of mystery to many students for some time in their studies. This chapter seeks to demystify notions of what critical thinking is (and isn't) by:

- Working towards a definition of critical thinking and supplying you with some practical examples.
- Showing you how to identify and analyse arguments in a piece of writing.
- Introducing ways to evidence critical thinking in your own writing.

Beginning to think critically

Being a student of Education requires you to approach information or perspectives you come across from an open point of view, and to position yourself well in order to exercise inquiry, interrogate the evidence you come across and then reflect upon a range of perspectives before coming to your own evidence-based judgement. Note that when we use the term 'critical thinking', this does not simply mean *criticising* what you come across – we present some differing definitions and encourage you to think about your own understanding of the term shortly.

Benchmarks, or expected standards for Education degree programmes, say that students should 'have opportunities to develop their critical capabilities through the *selection, analysis and synthesis of relevant perspectives*, and to be able to justify different positions on educational matters' (QAA, 2015, p. 6, our emphasis). The words in italics here are particularly significant, and go some way towards describing characteristics of critical thinking.

Definitions of critical thinking

Defining critical thinking can be problematic. You could ask ten tutors for their definition of critical thinking and they would all vary to a degree, with different interpretations or emphasis upon various aspects of critical thinking. Entering the term 'critical thinking' into a search engine brings up somewhere in the region of 80,000,000 results of differing definitions, online courses in critical thinking, guidance about how to think more critically in business and advice for students.

This is a good example of how using a general internet search to try and develop a definition of something quite complex can be problematic.

The definition that we would suggest is that ***critical thinking means engaging in objective, balanced and evidence-based analysis of an issue, in order to help us form sound judgements.***

So, applying a critical thinking approach to our studies requires that we:

- Acknowledge but then often put to one side our own subjective experiences or perspectives.
- Seek out a range of views on an issue to present a balanced appraisal of an issue or circumstances.
- Avoid making claims without having drawn on suitable evidence (see Chapter 2).
- Work towards offering some kind of final judgement or understanding of an issue based on our research, reflection, interpretation and discussion.

Implementing aspects of critical thinking into your work can be a way to further your understanding of complex issues and ideas, and a way to begin to reach for higher marks in your assessed work. It is highly likely that your course's programme specification or documentation describing the course refers to 'critical thinking' or something similar, just as can be seen in the QAA benchmark excerpt above. Critical thinking, or a variation of this (perhaps expressed slightly differently), is often also included as part of the assessment criteria for particular assignments in specific modules or units – for example, criticality or critical analysis.

A good way to begin to understand the way in which critical thinking can be part of your mindset, and something employed on a day-to-day basis, is through reviewing some scenarios in an educational context, as presented below:

1 Amina is in the second year of her Education programme and has two possible schools willing to host her for a placement. Both would be suitable, and valuable to her in terms of experience, but she needs to make a decision as to which would benefit her most in terms of personal and professional development.

2 Lewis began his degree studying both Education and Sociology. Towards the end of his first year he has the choice as to whether he should continue with both subjects or transfer to study only Education. He begins to research his options with both the next two years of his degree and his career aspirations in mind.

3 Sian is a newly qualified teacher in her first year with a Year 2 class. She has a meeting with a pupil's parents to discuss their son's behaviour, which has become a little challenging recently. Prior to the meeting she has to reflect upon the points she wants to get across, the parents' possible reactions and feelings, and identify some possible actions and positive ways forward.

4 Tayo is a support worker in a further education college who works with students with specific learning difficulties. Working with a student with dyslexia, he has to help them to identify the arguments they have presented in an essay and consider what kind of logical and justified conclusion they might present at the end of their work.

5 Sadiyah is a Special Educational Needs Co-ordinator (SENCO) in a primary school and is working to support class teachers with their inclusion of a new pupil who is on the

autistic spectrum. In consultation with other professionals, she is trying to identify which augmentative communication strategy for both pupils and teachers might be most appropriate, so that in addition to support from a teaching assistant, the pupil can experience greater social inclusion and work to build friendships.

These scenarios make it apparent that critical thinking is an everyday occurrence that is not only confined to academic studies, but is an approach and *way* of thinking that enables us to produce 'new' ways of thinking, perspectives, ideas, solutions or interpretations.

Below are three different definitions or viewpoints about critical thinking:

1 '[C]ritical thinking is the process of identifying what the argument is that is being put forward, and determining whether or not the premises justify accepting the conclusion (in other words, assessing whether it is a good argument or not' (Hanscomb, 2017, p. 5).
2 'Critical thinking means weighing up the arguments and evidence *for* and *against*' (Cottrell, 2008, p. 275, emphasis in original).
3 'The whole point of thinking critically is to find an appropriate response or a decision in a judgement' (Moon, 2008, p. 55).

ACTIVITY 5.1

Your own definition of critical thinking

The three perspectives above make it clear that critical thinking is not easy to define. Read each of the definitions again and then see if you can synthesise (bring the parts together) the points and take a few minutes to create your own definition of critical thinking …

Critical thinking is …

There is no right or wrong answer to this task, but regardless of what you have actually written as your definition, take a moment now to reflect and consider: *How did you go about doing the task?*

- Can you identify particular stages you went through in your thinking?
- Did you disregard any of the points put forward in favour of others?
- Did you make direct comparisons between the three perspectives?
- Did you identify what was missing from any or all of the views?
- Perhaps you concluded or made a judgement as to which perspective you prefer or find most useful, or which was the easiest to understand?
- Did you note down ideas and then reorganise or reword them into a more logical expression or sentence?
- Did it occur to you to question who the authors of these words are, and their credentials?

If any of these thoughts or processes were involved in your attempt to create your own definition of critical thinking, then *you have just engaged in the process of critical thinking yourself!*

Hopefully your own definition reflected some of the following key points:

- **Critical thinking requires a weighing up of evidence.**
- **Critical thinking requires us to challenge ideas.**
- **Critical thinking requires us to process and interrogate information in a logical manner.**
- **The conclusion or judgement that we arrive at can be supported or defended with the evidence we have used to come to that conclusion.**

A model commonly referred to in order to assist students' understanding of the *development* of academic skills is Bloom's Taxonomy, a model developed in the mid-twentieth century, and most commonly ascribed to Benjamin Bloom, published in 1956. You will undoubtedly come across and (hopefully!) engage in some critical thinking around the model itself throughout your time as an Education student, but in this chapter it is simply useful for us to refer to this model, as it is a good way to illustrate *progression* in thinking skills, with the lower levels of the model illustrating how students gain expertise gradually and as personal development in an area of study increases, the complexity of what the student is able to do with these ideas increases. This begins with having *knowledge* of something, working up to *comprehending* (understanding) this, *applying* it to new situations or problems, *analysing* it to examine the component parts, *synthesising* it in order to present the new outlook or interpretation, and lastly, *evaluating* the issue or information. It is the latter (higher) stages of this model from Bloom that can be described as critical thinking. See Chapter 9 for the commonly used image of Bloom's taxonomy, and also a link to a more contemporary model.

There aren't any kinds of 'quick fixes' or a set of rules you can implement to make your thinking, and subsequently your assessed work, more 'critical', but there are a number of habits or ways of thinking that you can try to adopt to help you be more receptive to the ideas and perspectives of others, and to begin to take a more critical stance. A few examples of these are outlined below briefly to begin to help you understand what we mean by 'critical thinking' and how you can work towards it:

- Keep up-to-date with educational news, developments, debates and policies so that you can draw on recent perspectives.
- Apply some of the points from Chapter 1 (to evaluate the provenance and credibility of sources) to all kinds of perspectives you come across.
- Be reluctant to simply 'accept' what you read without considering the possibility of other valid perspectives or points of view.
- Be prepared to engage with complexity rather than trying to seek out a simple or straightforward 'answer' or perspective to believe in.

Now that you have some ideas (and experience) about the concept of critical thinking, and what it might entail, the next part of this chapter examines some of the component parts, or skills, required for critical thinking in more depth.

Identifying and analysing arguments

What does the term 'argument' mean to you? In the first instance it might conjure up images of two people disagreeing with one another, perhaps in a heated manner, each trying to convey their own different views. In a more academic sense, an 'argument' can be thought of as reason (or reasons) as to why one particular point of view might be more important, weighty, significant or credible than another. A common task you might be given in your studies is identifying or evaluating arguments *for* or *against* particular perspectives, policies or strategies;

ACTIVITY 5.2

Identifying arguments in a piece of writing

The passage below is taken from a chapter about learners with Special Educational Needs and Disabilities (SEND), and the significance of labelling children with learning differences in an educational setting. Read this and then move on to the questions following it.

> Teachers, like all individuals, exercise a great deal of informal categorization or labelling. A teacher may, for example, note those learners that need additional help, those learners who are inattentive, those learners who are particularly keen, and so on. Each teacher may have a different set of informal categories and may apply them in a different way. At one end of the continuum these informal categories or 'labels' may be private to the teacher, and not shared with others. But even at this level, they may well influence how a teacher responds to a given child and influence their future perceptions of the child. At the next level, the teacher may more explicitly convey their categorization to the child or children in question or may share these labels with other teachers. A number of dyslexic children and older students are quite clear that some teachers call them 'lazy', 'stupid' or idiots (Riddick, 2010). Many teachers, in contrast, use largely helpful or constructive categories that enable them to target their teaching more effectively.

Source: Riddick, B. (2012) 'Labelling learners with 'SEND': The good, the bad and the ugly', in Armstrong, D. and Squires, G. (eds) *Contemporary Issues in Special Educational Needs*. Berkshire: Oxford University Press and McGraw-Hill Education, pp. 25–26.

Based only on your reading of this passage:

● Can you identify one argument FOR labelling children with SEND?

● Can you identify one argument AGAINST labelling children with SEND?

See suggested answers at the end of the chapter.

As a discipline rooted in the Social Sciences, it is essential to recognise that when analysing educational ideas there is never a point at which you will come to a 'correct' or 'final' point of view. Everything that we hear, read or are presented with is simply *a different perspective*, and it is the job of Education students to identify and then apply critical thinking to these arguments.

Once you have identified the arguments in a piece of text, the next step is to extend some analysis and critical thinking to the arguments you have identified. So, looking back to the definition or characteristics of critical thinking identified earlier in this chapter, we might pursue analysis of this issue by taking just one point, such as: *Labelling children with SEND can influence the way a teacher might respond to, or treat a child.*

The stages we would need to go through to interrogate this argument (or claim) would be:

1 **Weighing up evidence about this argument:** This would require researching and reviewing a number of different pieces of literature that have researched or written about this issue, and looking at their findings. Consideration should also be given to the provenance of the literature you're drawing upon, currency and the nature of evidence used to draw conclusions (remember the PROMPT mnemonic in Chapter 1).

2 **Challenging ideas about this argument:** It could be suggested that there is an assumption in this argument that teachers treating some children differently is always a negative thing, but it may actually be the case that, in line with requirements for educators to make reasonable adjustments for learners with SEND, labels can actually heighten awareness and tailor better teaching (thus contributing to our argument in *favour* of labelling children with SEND).

3 **Processing and interrogating information in a logical manner:** The way in which various evidence is considered needs to be in a structured and logical manner, which has implications for the organisation of your response/work. In order to allow people to recognise your critical thinking, your structure and the way in which you present and work through various perspectives and considerations need to be transparent.

4 **Arriving at a conclusion or judgement that can be supported or defended with the evidence we have used to come to that conclusion:** In a strong piece of academic writing it can be seen when various arguments are 'picked up', considered and then 'put down' again. Therefore, comments that make a judgement or demonstrate that some kind of decision has been reached in your thinking are a good way to illustrate your critical thinking. For example,

you might end a discussion by saying: 'It is apparent from the discussions presented here that there is a limited amount of evidence available to support this particular viewpoint.' Note here that this doesn't mean you need to come to a definitive statement in favour of one side of an argument or another – remember that there aren't 'right' or 'wrong' answers in the Social Sciences; conclusions need to be clearly based on the evidence you've presented and leave the reader with your final judgement.

So, the guidance above supplies you with some insight into how a piece of text you read might be approached from a more critical perspective. This is reinforced by the guidance supplied by Cottrell (2008, p. 276) who suggests that critical thinking when reading requires:

1 Identifying the line of reasoning in the text.
2 Critically evaluating the line of reasoning.
3 Questioning surface appearances and checking for hidden assumptions or agendas.
4 Identifying evidence in the text.
5 Evaluating the evidence according to valid criteria.
6 Identifying the writer's conclusion.
7 Deciding whether the evidence given supports these conclusions.

Showing critical thinking in your writing

So far this chapter has encouraged you to adopt the mindset of an enquiring Education student, and to be more sceptical and systematic in your reading. The next steps are to think about how you can make your own writing display more critical thinking.

ACTIVITY 5.3

Identifying critical thinking in written work

The following section illustrates a task given to students, which was to present an overview of two sources and then enter into a brief discussion comparing the findings of each. Read through the student's work below and then consider the questions that follow.

Source 1: Crowley, C., Hallam, S., Harre, R. and Lunt, I. (2003) 'Peer support for people with same-sex attraction', in Nind, M., Sheehy, K. and Simmons, K. (eds) *Inclusive Education: Learners and Learning Contexts*. London: David Fulton Publishers.

> *This chapter recounts the findings of research carried out with a small number of 15- to 16-year-old pupils in the late 1990s in Manchester – hence it is fair to say this is now a somewhat dated perspective. Through interviews with the young people, researchers found that insults, isolation, fear and prejudice were all common experiences which caused a great deal of distress and pressure throughout schooling. Consequently, all agreed that there had been a severe impact upon their education as they were inclined to attend less, and there were difficult times communicating with the school and trying*

to get support – some even moved schools. The research then looked at their experiences of a Peer Support Project and found that their involvement with this had been positive, creating a safe space for them to access study support and helping them to cope at school.

Source 2: Rivers, I. and Cowie, H. (2006) 'Bullying and homophobia in UK schools: A perspective on factors affecting resilience and recovery', *Journal of Gay & Lesbian Issues in Education*, Vol. 3, No. 4, pp. 11–43.

> This journal article reports on the findings of a three-year study with people who were victimized in their school days due to their sexuality. Early on in the article, the authors review what has already been written in this area and refer to a number of studies that have previously identified homophobic bullying in the UK, so it is clear this is not a new problem. By gathering data through two questionnaires and interviews, the researchers found that individuals had consistently experienced bullying over many years throughout their education, most frequently name calling, but also physical abuse, fear, isolation and even sexual assault. They also concluded that the kind of social support offered at school (if any) had been important, and 'acted as a buffer' (Rivers and Cowie, 2006, p. 33)

Discussion by student:

These two studies both supply convincing evidence that pupils who identify as gay or lesbian experience discrimination in their schooling, despite their very different approaches. Crowley et al.'s study was of a small scale but in-depth nature which gathered qualitative data (interviews) about experiences that had occurred relatively recently for the participants. In contrast, Rivers and Cowie's participants were aged 16–66, and so many were reporting on experiences from several decades ago, and this should be taken into account as social attitudes and awareness towards sexuality are ever-changing. It was also a much larger scale study, with 190 participants.

Both studies identified some common negative experiences of bullying, verbal and physical, as a result of having a different sexuality. Insults, name calling, fear of walking home alone and being beaten up were all experienced by one pupil in Crowley et al.'s study who said that 'All the grief I get is sexually oriented' (2003, p. 117). Participants in Rivers and Cowie's study also identified these experiences, but added that they had also been subjected to having their belongings stolen and even sexual assault.

The consequences of such victimization at school were found to have a lasting impact in both studies. Rivers and Cowie found that fifty-three per cent of pupils said they had self-harmed as a result of the bullying (2006, p. 25), and that seventeen per cent displayed symptoms of Post-Traumatic Stress Disorder, a psychological condition that according to De Bellis (2001) can have a significant impact upon linguistic, social, behavioural and cognitive skills. This is demonstrated through the experience of Mark, a participant in Crowley et al.'s study, who recalls being in class once when the teacher left, and other pupils quickly starting to taunt him. As a result of this he says, 'I … totally switched off and went into my own little world and didn't come out of it again till

3.30 when the bell rang' (2003, p. 180). This lack of engagement at school then progressed to him truanting and missing nearly half of school across one term.

Discrimination on the grounds of sexuality is illegal and this was incorporated into the Equality Act (2010). However, legislation cannot govern behaviour, and so schools should consider what they can do to try and tackle this, just as they have been trying to do with regard to racism since the 1990s.

Now read through the text in the box again, and **try to reflect on the extent to which the work illustrates evidence of critical thinking**, using these prompts:

1   Can you identify where the writer is making any judgements or decisions about particular issues or points under consideration? Do you feel these judgements have been reached through sufficient consideration and comparison of both sources?

2   Are there clear lines of reasoning? That is, can you see where the writer's thinking, logic and rationale for the points they're making are apparent?

3   Is there evidence (in addition to the two sources being compared) supplied to support claims that are made? Is the kind of evidence used appropriate and sufficient?

4   Is there evidence of a questioning approach, where it is apparent that the writer is being sceptical or analytical?

5   Lastly, can you identify any ways in which it might be improved in order to demonstrate more critical thinking?

The text is supplied below again with some additional comments and annotations to help you recognise what would be considered as strengths to this piece of writing, and what areas would benefit from more attention:

Source 1: Crowley, C., Hallam, S., Hare, R. and Lunt, I. (2003) 'Peer support for people with same-sex attraction' in Nind, M., Sheehy, K. and Simmons, K. (eds) (2003) *Inclusive Education: Learners and Learning Contexts* London: David Fulton Publishers Ltd.

Useful comment upon characteristics of the research in terms of sample size and date

This chapter recounts the findings of research carried out with a small number of 15 to 16-year-old pupils in the late 1990s in Manchester – hence it is fair to say this is now a somewhat dated perspective. Through interviews with the young people, researchers found that insults, isolation, fear and prejudice were all common experiences which caused a great deal of distress and pressure throughout schooling. Consequently, all agreed that there had been a severe impact upon their education as they were inclined to attend less, and there were difficult times communicating with the school and trying to get support – some even moved schools. The research then looked at their experiences of a Peer Support Project and found that their involvement with this had been positive, creating a safe space for them to access study support and helping them to cope at school.

Source 2: Rivers, I. and Cowie, H. (2006) 'Bullying and Homophobia in UK schools: A perspective on factors affecting resilience and recovery' *Journal of Gay & Lesbian Issues in Education* Vol. 3 Issue 4 pp. 11–43

This journal article reports on the findings of a three-year study with people who were victimized in their school days due to their sexuality. Early on in the article, the authors review what has already been written in this area and refer to a number of studies that have previously identified homophobic bullying in the UK, so it is clear this is not a new problem. By gathering data through two questionnaires and interviews, the researchers found that individuals had consistently experienced bullying over many years throughout their education, most frequently name calling, but also physical abuse, fear, isolation and even sexual assault. They also concluded that the kind of social support offered at school (if any) had been important, and "acted as a buffer" (Rivers and Cowie 2006:33).

This comment indicates the writer has thought about the authors' rationale for their research

Discussion:

A key claim by the writer, evidenced by the overview of each source above

These two studies both supply convincing evidence that pupils who identify as gay or lesbian experience discrimination in their schooling, despite their very different approaches. Crowley et al.'s study was of a small scale but in-depth nature which gathered qualitative data (interviews) about experiences that had occurred relatively recently for the participants. In contrast, Rivers and Cowie's participants were aged from 16–66, and so many were reporting on experiences from several decades ago, and this should be taken into account as social attitudes and awareness towards sexuality are ever changing. It was also a much larger scale study, with 190 participants.

Highlights limitations and strengths (balanced)

What's missing here is an explanation as to why this might be significant. It's not clear whether this is being presented as a positive or negative aspect of the research

Clear identification of commonality, evidenced by the two examples in this paragraph

Both studies identified some common negative experiences of bullying, verbal and physical as a result of having a different sexuality. Insults, name calling, fear of walking home alone and being beaten up were all experienced by one pupil in Crowley et al.'s study who said that "All the grief I get is sexually oriented" (2003:117). Participants in Rivers and Cowie's study also identified these experiences, but added that they had also been subjected to having their belongings stolen and even sexual assault.

Evidence again from each study to support the claim in the first sentence

The consequences of such victimization at school were found to have a lasting impact in both studies. Rivers and Cowie found that fifty three per cent of pupils said they had self-harmed as a result of the bullying (2006:25), and that seventeen per cent displayed symptoms of Post-Traumatic Stress Disorder, a psychological condition that according to De Bellis (2001) can have a significant impact upon linguistic, social, behavioural and cognitive skills. This is demonstrated through the experience of Mark, a participant in Crowley et al.'s study, who recalls being in class once when the teacher left, and other pupils quickly starting to taunt him. As a result of this he says, "I...totally switched off and went into my own little world and didn't come out of it again till 3.30 when the bell rang" (2003:180). This lack of engagement at school then progressed to him truanting and missing nearly half of school across one term.

Show logic in this discussion: a 'problem' has been established, some evidence has been presented, examining the consequences is the next step

A comment that recognises the complexity of this issue

Discrimination on the grounds of sexuality is illegal and this has been incorporated into the recent Equality Act (2010) which applies to educational settings. However, legislation cannot govern behaviour, and so schools should consider what they can do to try and tackle this, just as they have been trying to do with regard to racism since the 1990s.

Bit of a disappointing, throwaway line here: what have schools been doing with regard to racism?

Fairly logical to then consider the legal/policy perspective here. Reference to relevant legislation

Chapter summary: useful points for you to implement

- Remember that critical thinking is a contested concept: expect to spend time engaged in exploratory discussions and activities to experience critical thinking. Accept it will take a while before you might feel you've grasped it.
- Critical thinking is a mindset and approach rather than a discrete skill.
- Prioritise challenging ideas, exercising scepticism and working towards making evidence-based judgements.

Answers to Activity 5.2

Your answers might have included:

Arguments FOR labelling children with SEND	Arguments AGAINST labelling children with SEND
Can help teachers to be aware of learners that might need extra support	Can influence the way a teacher might respond to, or treat a child
Can help teachers to teach more effectively	Can influence their future perceptions (and perhaps expectations) of a child
	Children may become aware of these labels and be impacted negatively by them

Writing as an Education Student

Planning Your Writing

The following information in this chapter and subsequent chapters will help you to understand what's involved with academic writing at university. Like with painting or sculpting, writing is a skilled process that takes time and practise to develop.

Planning your writing is perhaps the most important stage of the academic writing process. You may have not needed to plan the writing of your assignments in previous stages of your education but as Lecturers in Education we would strongly encourage you to plan your work at university. You'll need to organise all your thoughts and ideas that you've been learning about and developing from your research and reading and planning will help you to do this.

Students who are new to studying Education and writing assignments often misread or misunderstand what they are being asked to do, and instead of focusing on a particular aspect or requirement they take the 'write everything I know about the subject approach' and write broadly about the topic. Planning is important because the task enables you to break down the writing process into necessary stages and to check your progress at various points – for example, 'Do I understand the task?' and 'Am I answering the question?'. In this chapter we take a look at:

- The stages of planning and writing, beginning with the crucial question 'What is the task?'.
- Time management and how much time is needed to produce an assignment.
- Some effective strategies to help you to develop an argument in your writing.

Firstly, what's the task?

Before you begin planning what you are going to write about you need to make sure that you fully understand what the task is asking you to do so that you can address and answer the question. As Norton and colleagues (2009, p. 46) state, 'addressing the question is the main objective of an essay assignment, and how well you can do this has a direct relationship to the grade you will get'. Assignment task briefs or questions can often be quite long and confusing so breaking them down into chunks that are more manageable to unpack and understand them is often helpful.

The types of words in assignment questions and task briefs are often described as 'content' and 'command' words. Content words give you information about what the topic of your assignment should focus on and the command words give you the instructions regarding what you should do in the assignment, such as

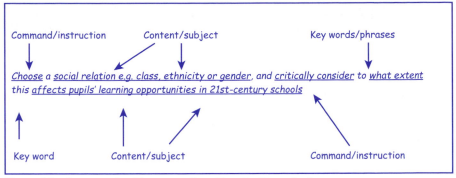

Figure 6.1   An example of 'command' and 'content' words diagram

describe the role of a practitioner or *critically compare* two theories. The task of describing is different to a critical comparison and the writing will be different.

In the example in Figure 6.1 the significant parts of the question have been underlined and they help to form the basis of the essay plan.

If you do not understand any part of the question/task brief you should ask your lecturer or peers. You may find that some of your class friends are also having difficulty understanding the task so talking about it together and breaking down the task may help you all to understand.

Some tasks at university, particularly in the later years of study (e.g. second and third years and postgraduate study), ask students to create their own titles for assignments (see Activity 6.1 for an example). To do this you need to build the title up rather than break it down, so it's like completing the previous process in reverse! Often you will need to think about what topic you would like to write about and some reasons why you are interested in this subject area(s). You will also need to decide what you will do in the assignment and what the focus of your argument will be – for example, will you evaluate, critically evaluate, define, outline or critically compare what the subject focus of your writing is? To make this decision you should also remind yourself of the module/course and university assessment criteria because you will typically achieve a higher grade if you critically engage with ideas, theories and concepts in your writing and do this to an appropriate level as outlined by the marking criteria.

ACTIVITY 6.1

Task brief for a critical essay

Identify a contemporary issue that can influence the educational experiences of children and young people and the various transitions that they may take into adulthood. You should create your own title (with guidance from the tutor). Your arguments need to discuss issues around key themes relating to children and young people, education, risk and their transitions to adulthood.

For this assignment, you are expected to:

1   Draw on key concepts and ideas developed during the module (e.g. issues of risk, gender, academic achievement, identity) as you critically discuss the contemporary issue(s) that you have identified.

2   Draw on relevant journal articles and other academic resources to develop your argument(s) and discuss the issues.

3   Consider the implications of this contemporary issue and research for education and/or educational practitioners.

Time management: how long will it take?

It always takes longer than you think it will! When you have an assessment deadline remember that writing an assignment is a process. There's a lot more involved than just writing the assignment. You will need to understand the question, think about the argument you would like to present (we'll look at this later in the chapter), reread your lecture and seminar notes and then find wider reading before refining your argument(s) and presenting it in a coherent structure. You then need to leave enough time to proofread and edit your work. This final part of the process is often the one students tend to forget about until it's too late and there's not enough time before the deadline. Considering this process and allowing time for the unexpected (you never know what might happen), it is advisable to 'work backwards' from the deadline and realistically think about what you can do in the time available to you. Remember you may need to plan your reading, researching and writing around family, childcare or a job. A week may sound like a long time to write an essay but when you factor in other university work, working, cooking and eating, sleeping, socialising and doing chores such as laundry there perhaps are not as many hours in a day as you would like (or need)!

Instead, break the work down into smaller steps and 'chunk' the tasks as this will make it more manageable. Here is a suggested outline of a step-by-step approach for a typical essay type task.

An eight-step plan

1   Read and reread the information about the assignment task

2   What is the question asking?

3   Create a plan

4   Research, read and do more research

5   Check your plan – think about the structure and ask yourself 'Am I answering the question?'

6   Do more reading

7   Draft

8   Take a break and then come back to your work with 'fresh eyes' to proofread and edit

1   **Read and reread the information about the assignment task**
    Make sure you have all the important information about submitting the
    assignment – for example, the time and date that the assignment needs to be
    submitted and whether you need to hand in a hard copy or submit it
    electronically. This is very important because at university you can lose marks on
    assignments that are submitted later than the deadline (unless you have an
    extension granted).

2   **What is the question asking?**
    Once you have the deadline and submission information it is essential to focus on
    the task and what the question is asking you. As we mentioned earlier in this
    chapter you will gain more marks for specifically answering the question. Taking
    the 'let's write everything we know about a topic' approach will not get you
    marks. Once you've broken down the question and identified the command and
    content words, if you're still unsure about what you're being asked to do, ask your
    lecturer for clarification. You need to have thought about the task, though, and
    you will get more information from your questioning if you ask specific questions
    rather than just saying 'help! I don't understand' to your lecturer.

3   **Create a plan**
    Using your lecture and seminar notes create a rough plan to guide you with your
    reading and research. Some questions to get you started with creating a plan
    include:

    ● What general topic are you focusing on?
    ● What are the mini areas of research that you need to focus on? You may need
      to look through your lecture and seminar notes to identify these.
    ● Why is this topic important to you and Education?
    ● What do you already know about the topic?
    ● What are your initial thoughts – what do you want to say?
    ● What do you think you should know more about for the assignment?
    ● What literature/key theories, concepts and ideas will help you to support your
      argument? – remember this can include positive appraisals as well as
      negative ones.
    ● What conclusion would you like to make?

    At this stage, it's also a good idea to check your ideas for the assignment
    alongside the assessment criteria and your university's or course's marking criteria.
    For example, ask yourself whether the topic area and writing you intend to do will
    ensure that you can demonstrate knowledge, understanding and evidence of
    critical thinking as well as a good level of overall scholarship to gain higher marks.
    You could also create an annotated bibliography and make a note of key
    references alongside key points (see the next section about essay plans).

4   **Research, read and do more research**
    When you're clear about the task you need to do, you need to read, make notes,
    read and make more notes (if you need a recap about academic reading and
    taking effective notes please look at Chapters 2 and 3). Note down direct quotes
    and paraphrase sections when reading. When you're reading it's important to
    make a note of all of the bibliographic information about the text you're reading –

for example, an author's surname and initial(s), the date of publication, the title of the piece and the title of the book or article if it is from one of these sources as well as information about the publisher's name and the place of publication. It is also useful to note, well essential if you're intending to use a direct quotation, to make a note of the page number that the text is from. You can also save time by organising the references from your reading as you go along rather than leaving the referencing task until you've written the assignment. This will also ensure that you're not frantically looking for referencing information at the last minute.

5 **Check your plan – think about the structure and ask yourself 'Am I answering the question?'**
Are you addressing and answering the question? You should continue to ask yourself these questions during the planning and researching process. It's important to make sure that the literature you're reading and the references you've collected help you to support your viewpoints and the arguments you're making. When you're considering if you're answering the question, think about whether or not you've got enough depth to your argument. Remember your lecturers are not interested in reading everything you know about a topic. Instead, you should be focusing on the detail and depth of one topic or perhaps even one aspect of a topic.

6 **Do more reading**
Depending on your responses to the questions in 'chunk 5', you may need to do more reading and this is perfectly fine (as long as you've left enough time to complete the task)! When you're reviewing your plan, consider whether you have enough depth to your writing and enough wider reading, perhaps different viewpoints and/or approaches to the topic(s) you're focusing on.

7 **Draft**
Everyone will plan and draft their work differently. You may have been drafting your ideas and developing your writing as you've been reading so at this point you should write a complete draft. This will help you to see the overall structure and the development of the arguments within your writing.

8 **Take a break and then come back to your work with 'fresh eyes' to proofread and edit**
Once you have a draft of your work you should leave it for a period of time before coming back to it with a fresh pair of eyes. The amount of time available to you will depend on when you started to plan and write the assignment. As you can see, there can be a number of tasks to writing an assignment so hopefully you will begin an assignment well in advance of the deadline so that you can leave your work for a day or two before proofreading it. However, if you don't have this much time available try and allow for a break of at least a couple of hours.

The proofreading and editing stage is important because doing these tasks will allow you to spot and correct any mistakes and make improvements to your writing. The reason we suggest you take a break from your writing before doing this is so that you can have a fresh look at your work and pay particular close attention to:

- The structure – for example, are your introductory and concluding paragraphs clear?
- The way the argument develops throughout your writing

- The way you've used the literature to evidence and support your points – do you need to include more references to strengthen your viewpoint(s)?
- The spelling, punctuation and grammar of your writing.

Taking a break from your writing means that you are more likely to spot mistakes because you're not as familiar with the text as you are when you've just finished writing. The following tips may help you to proofread effectively:

- Read your assignment out loud
- Put each sentence on a new line
- Read your assignment backwards, starting with the last word on each page.

You could also ask a friend or family member to look at your draft because they may spot something that you have missed. They may not have an understanding of the content but they can pick up errors – for example, with communication and/or spelling – and let you know whether your work makes sense or not.

A student's perspective: 'Milestone Motivations'

Breaking the task into chunks also allows you to create motivational milestones. Once you have reached a particular milestone e.g. finished researching the application of a theory or your reference list you can have a treat.

(BA Education Graduate)

Different ways to plan your essays

An essay plan is important because it helps you to organise and structure your ideas. There are various approaches to organising your ideas – for example, a mind map, headings and bullet points, an annotated bibliography. The main thing is that the approach to planning you use helps you with your writing process to enable you to write the assignment. Figure 6.2 presents an example for you to try.

Claire Williams, a BA Education Graduate, prefers to plan her ideas using a mind map because it helps her to see the strands of thinking within and between the themes of her ideas. It also helps her to illustrate the links between the themes. Claire said this enables her to visualise the structure of an assignment and see any patterns emerging – for example, with the literature to support the arguments being made.

Headings and bullet points (with annotated bibliography)

Some students prefer to work in a more linear fashion with text, as illustrated in Box 6.1. An annotated bibliography includes key references to help build an argument.

Every student will have their own personal viewpoints about which type of plans are most accessible and useful to them. Although there is much heated debate in the Educational Research literature about whether learning styles exist or if they are a myth (see Li et al., 2016), every learner will have a preference for a particular approach to planning essay writing.

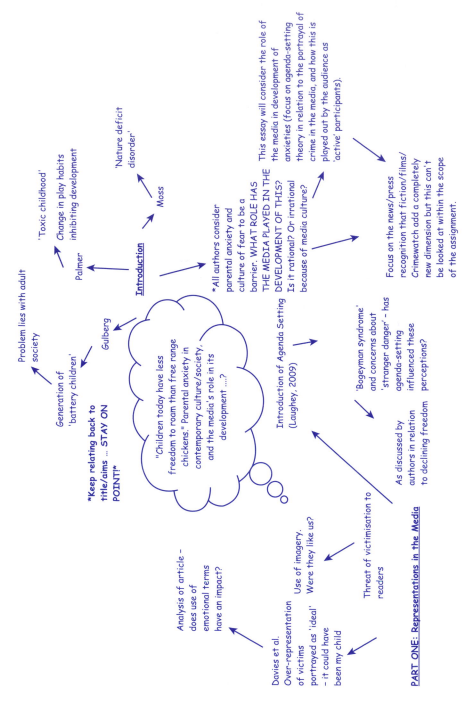

Figure 6.2 An example mind map diagram

Box 6.1   An example of a student's work in progress Essay title/topic

'Children today have less freedom to roam than free range chickens.' Parental anxiety in contemporary culture/society, and the media's role in its development …?

Introduction

- All authors consider parental anxiety and culture of fear to be a barrier … What role has the media played in the development of this? Is it rational? Or irrational as a result of media culture?
- Gulberg – Generation of 'battery' children and adult culture of fear holding children back.
- Palmer – 'toxic childhood' (change in play habits inhibiting development).
- Moss – 'Nature deficit disorder'.
- This essay will consider the role of the media in development of anxieties (focus on agenda-setting theory in relation to the portrayal of crime in the media), and how this is played out by the audience as 'active' participants.
- Focus on the news/press recognition that fiction/films/crimewatch add a completely new dimension but this can't be looked at within the scope of the assignment.

Representation in the media

- Introduction of agenda-setting theory (Laughey, 2009)
  - ○ 'Bogeyman syndrome' and concerns about 'stranger danger' – has agenda-setting influenced these perceptions? – Explore this concept in this section.
- Jewkes (2004)
  - ○ ideas about mis/over/underrepresentation – official statistics and representation in the media and newsworthiness
  - ○ Influencing images of crime in the media
- Threat of victimisation
  - ○ threat to readers (Davies et al., 2008) e.g. 'it could have been my child'
- Moral panic?
  - ○ As a result of agenda-setting? Framing an issue in a certain way?
  - ○ Causes audience to change behaviours
  - ○ Role of the media?

Conclusion

The agenda set by media in relation to crime is shaping public perceptions about the likelihood of their child being a victim of 'stranger danger'.

- Jewkes (2004) – media as a 'prism' rather than a window on the world
- But there's an assumption the audience are passive recipients rather than constructing meaning.

Developing an argument in your writing

To begin developing an argument we must understand what an argument actually is. It is *your* response to the question or task you've been asked to answer, the statement of what you think about a particular topic *supported* by relevant literature and sources. It should be the central starting point of your assignment and it will help to determine your reading, the evidence you collect and draw upon, the quotations you use and the structure of your writing.

The starting point for developing an argument is to recognise what it should look like. Creme and Lea (2008, p. 83) describe constructing an argument as similar to writing a story with a plot, a beginning, a middle and an end. They highlight that, as a student writer, a student should write their 'story-argument so that it is convincing for the tutor/reader' (Creme and Lea, 2008, p. 83). We find this analogy between an argument and a story useful because having a storyline helps us to ensure we are answering the assignment question or addressing the task brief.

What's your perspective?

Before you can start to build your argument, you need to consider what your perspective is in relation to the question or task you've been asked to complete. To do this you also need to consider all of the perspectives that are available to you, even if they vary, and both sides of the argument (these may be called claims and counter-claims in the literature) before you come to your own position, your conclusion. As we've mentioned before, you could also make sure that you are answering the question. In addition to the process we outlined earlier in the book, some helpful questions to get you started are:

- What do you agree with?
- What are you going to be arguing for?
- What supporting evidence do you have?

ACTIVITY 6.2

Identifying arguments

Read the following statements. What are the claims/arguments and counter-claims/arguments for the following questions or statements?

- 'Children with Special Educational Needs should be educated in mainstream schools'. To what extent do you agree with this statement?
- Choose a learning theorist, e.g. Piaget or Vygotsky, and critically discuss the implications of their theory in twenty-first century classrooms.

For the first question, *'Children with Special Educational Needs should be educated in mainstream schools'. To what extent do you agree with this statement?* Your answers might have included:

Claim: Children with Special Educational Needs should be educated in mainstream schools.

Counter-argument/claim: Children with Special Educational Needs should not be educated in mainstream schools.

You should also consider the 'to what extent' aspect of the question and it is asking you to consider whether you agree with the statement or not. You might have come up with the following responses to this part of the question:

- Children with Special Educational Needs should be educated in mainstream schools to a great extent.
- Children with Special Educational Needs should be educated in mainstream schools to a lesser extent.
- Some children with Special Educational Needs should be educated in mainstream schools and other children should be taught in complex needs schools because there are many perspectives to consider.

For the second task, 'Choose a learning theorist, e.g. Piaget or Vygotsky, and critically discuss the implications of the theory for learning in twenty-first century classrooms' you might have thought about claims similar to the following:

Claim: The implications of Piaget's or Vygotsky's theory of learning development (depending on which theorist you choose) help us to understand learning in twenty-first century classrooms.

Counter-argument/claims: (1) The implications of Piaget's or Vygotsky's theory of learning development (depending on which theorist you choose) does not help us to understand learning in twenty-first century classrooms; (2) The implications of Piaget's and Vygotsky's theories of learning development each contribute towards an understanding of learning in twenty-first century classrooms.

Building upon an argument: supporting your claims

Once you have decided on your claim and your developing line of argument you need to demonstrate, illustrate and support it with evidence from relevant literature and wider reading in a logical manner. Your reader will need to be persuaded to accept the claim you're making or to see how the claim is substantiated. Therefore, this evidence needs to be good (refer back to Chapter 1 where we discuss the different types of sources and which ones can be considered as 'academic'). As well as supporting your arguments with good evidence from the wider literature, you should also support them in appropriate places in your text and provide a context.

ACTIVITY 6.3

Evaluating arguments

Read the text below and consider if the writer has presented a clear argument:

The inclusion of Sex and Relationship Education (SRE) in the National Curriculum has received increasing attention from researchers, educators and policy makers. Schools where SRE has been explicitly and regularly taught have reported young people have a better understanding of sexual relationships and emotions. Figures also show that such an approach is also likely to delay sexual activity in young people. There have however been more recent surveys researching young people's voices which present a very different, and more worrying situation.

What questions might a reader ask which would suggest a weak argument?

- Where is the evidence that there is a link between SRE curriculum/lesson and young people's understanding of sex, relationships and emotions?
- What do we mean by 'a better understanding'?
- What figures?

Including your perspective

Depending on the assessment, it may be appropriate to draw on your own experiences to demonstrate a particular point. The advantage of including your own perspective is that it gives your writing a more personal touch and it enables you to demonstrate an understanding of the links between educational practices and literature. However, you need to make sure that your tone remains academic and you avoid phrases such as 'I think' and 'I believe'. You should ground any anecdotes you draw on to illustrate a point within relevant academic sources, and therefore you're constructing an argument which goes beyond your thoughts and opinions. We will look at reflecting on your own experiences and drawing on these in your writing in Chapters 11 and 12.

Chapter summary: useful points for you to implement

- Make sure you answer the essay question and/or address the task brief.
- Break the writing process into manageable 'chunks'.
- Make sure you plan and draft your writing.
- Start your essay writing process well in advance of the deadline to make sure you leave enough time to proofread and edit your work to be able to improve it.
- Consider using 'motivational milestones' to support you with the writing process.

The Characteristics of Academic Writing

At university, students are required to write 'academically' for a number of different assignments, namely the traditional essay, but also in presentations for example, so it's a good idea to learn about and understand the characteristics of academic writing. In this chapter we will explore the following to give you guidance to help you understand academic writing at university:

- What makes a piece of work 'academic'?
- The language and style of academic writing – Can I use 'I'?
- Understanding assessment criteria.

Firstly, before we go any further we would like to crush a common myth about academic writing and writing at university. It is not about using big words that you do not understand and then putting them into complicated sentences that do not make sense to the reader. Instead, it is about communication – communicating particular ideas and arguments to your reader. To do this you need to articulate your thoughts, to think about what you have learned in lectures, discussed in seminars and discovered in your wider reading. In your assignments you will then demonstrate this as *understanding*. Within the discipline of Education you could be asked to present an argument, or apply a particular theoretical approach to practice, and to then support it with 'evidence' from research and other literature before making conclusions and giving recommendations (if the task/assignment brief asks for this). Supporting your points with evidence as part of your argument is key as it will help you to demonstrate your knowledge and understanding while also convincing your reader of the claims you're making.

What makes a piece of work 'academic'? Language, style and structure

Academic writing is a particular way of writing and communicating ideas and arguments to a reader, lecturer and marker. As Lillis and Turner (2001) highlight, it is rooted in a western historical-cultural model where writing is the smooth transition of ideas and arguments which are referenced from other writers' work. It tends to be more formal (e.g. you should not contract expressions such as 'don't', 'can't', 'won't', 'didn't' and you should avoid using colloquial language or slang terms) and it is often impersonal in nature – for example, of the reporting and presenting of ideas and theories rather than only writing about your own personal views. However, within Education Studies, critical reflection practices and reflective writing are very important and we'll look at this more closely in Chapters 11 and 12. The key word in the previous sentence is 'critical'.

A good way to learn about academic writing in Education subjects is to study the language, style and structure used within journal articles. When you are reading for your lectures and seminars, some key points to consider are:

- What is the structure? How does the author begin and close a paragraph? How do they link between paragraphs?
- What language has the author used? Does it sound formal and more objective? What words and phrases have they utilised to achieve this? What style is it written in? It is very unlikely for an author to use phrases such as 'I think' or 'in my opinion'. Instead, you will probably notice phrases such as 'it can be argued' or 'the authors consider'. It is also uncommon for the writing to be casual – for example, written down in a way that is similar to spoken language.

ACTIVITY 7.1

Identifying academic style

See if you can spot the differences between these two example texts discussing testing in schools and the notion of 'fear of failure' (Jackson, 2006). Consider which one is more academic and make a note of your reasons for your choices.

Example 1

I think the fear of failure has cropped up within recent years as children are becoming more anxious about the SATs with many of them facing anxieties around the fear of failing due to all the pressure that the tests are causing.

Example 2

Earlier research studies suggest that there is a long-standing link between SATs and anxiety in pupils (Reay and Wiliam, 1999). More recently, Alexander (2010) has illustrated that children are continuing to feel anxious about testing. Jackson (2013) has explored this increasing anxiety and the notion of 'fear of failure'.

Noticeably, the style is different. As we mentioned earlier, academic writing tends to be written in an objective and impersonal way. The tone in Example 1 is not considered academic because the writer has used phrases such as 'I think that' and 'cropped up'. There is no need to write phrases like these or others such as 'in my opinion' because as the author it is clear what you think from your writing and you need to present more than your opinion in your writing. You may start with an opinion when you begin reading and researching for the assignment but this will develop into your argument because you will present your viewpoint and support it with evidence from the literature. Eventually you will have reasoned arguments and you should present them in an objective way while drawing on peer-reviewed and relevant literature to support them.

As you may have noticed while reading journal articles and other Education literature, there are some variations in style. This is also the case for the Schools and Departments of Education in different universities. Some lecturers prefer students to adopt a more impersonal and subjective style to writing and it will very much depend on the task (as we mentioned earlier about reflective writing). If you're unsure of the approach to style within your university, make sure you ask your lecturers. Here are some questions that may help you find out about the characteristics of academic writing for your course, and which approach your School/ Department of Education uses:

- Can I use 'I' or should I write in the third person (e.g. 'the researcher')?
- Can I include my personal experiences? And should I support this with evidence from relevant literature?
- What tense should I use to write my assignment?
- Can I use bullet points?
- Can I use subheadings?

TIP

For more detailed guidance on writing sentences and paragraphs, we would recommend *Brilliant Writing Tips for Students* by Julia Copus (2009). This is full of very practical advice about punctuation, sentence and paragraph structure and academic style.

Looking back at the two examples, the language used is also different and the second piece of text has a greater command of the literature. The work is presented in a way which illustrates they have an understanding of the work of the author being referred to (Alexander, 2010). To help you with your writing it's a good idea to build up a vocabulary word bank of all the words and phrases you hear in lectures, read in texts and discuss in seminars. If you're unsure about what they mean do some research or ask your lecturer. Some of our students have identified words and phrases that they often use in their writing and in Box 7.1 we've started a list for you.

Box 7.1   Sample Vocabulary Bank

Achievement – A learner's performance or attainment.

Attainment – A learner's level of progress as defined by criteria – for example, SATs and GCSEs.

Constructivism – Learning is an active process where learners create new knowledge from existing understanding. Piaget was a key theorist.

Socioconstructivism – Learning is socially and culturally constructed and interaction with others is important. Vygotsky was a key theorist.

Discourse – A collection of ideas, knowledge, thoughts and ways of knowing.

Pedagogy – The study of learning and teaching.

Curriculum – A series of content to be covered and taught. A set of ideas. Often linked to learning outcomes and assessment.

Inclusion – Educating and supporting everyone to participate fully in society. Being respective of difference and values. Providing a supportive environment.

Capital – Key idea from Pierre Bourdieu. There are different forms of capital – for example, 'social', 'economic', 'cultural' and 'symbolic'. They are often linked to social class and distributed unequally.

Paradigm – A particular view, way of thinking, about ideas and concepts.

Academic writing + addressing criteria = a good assignment

Now that you have an understanding of what academic writing looks like, you also need to make sure you understand the ways in which your assignments will be assessed. It is important for you to know what criteria your lecturers and/or tutors will use to assess your work and how it will be marked. Research studies have illustrated that it is important for you to know what your task is and to understand the assessment criteria because there can be mismatches between students' and lecturers' perceptions about the most important criteria (Norton, 1990). During the 1990s and 2000s Lin Norton and her colleagues highlighted that tutors were often concerned with argument and students were concerned with content in the marking of assignments (Norton et al., 1996a, 1996b, Itua et al., 2014) and they developed the basic core assessment criteria for essay writing:

- Answering the question
- Structuring the assignment
- Demonstrating understanding
- Developing an argument
- Using evidence
- Evaluating sources
- Use of written language.

(Norton et al., 2009).

Although this will vary from subject to subject and institution to institution, knowledge about the answers to such questions will enable you to write your assignments. If you're unsure you should ask your lecturers, tutors and or other students, perhaps those who are in the years above you. A BA Education Graduate has the following advice:

A student's perspective: Thoughts on the characteristics of academic writing

The characteristics of academic writing are: 'Understanding the breadth of literature already surrounding your topic, as well as being able to highlight specific key points within this literature. Once this understanding has been gained, you can then begin to consider your own personal viewpoints against the literature. Be critical, be honest ... use both your reading of the literature as well as personal experience to explore the topic you're writing about.'

(Aimee, Year 3 BA Education student)

Chapter summary: useful points for you to implement

- Academic writing is more formal than everyday language, but it doesn't need to have big words you don't understand and long convoluted sentences (unless it is terminology).
- Remember that your institution may have academic support services to help you with study skills, such as workshops on structuring and planning work, literature searching or avoiding plagiarism. Be sure to find out about these and make use of them.

8

Structuring and Beginning Your Writing

Oftentimes, actually committing text to a document to begin writing an assessed piece of work can be daunting. Chapter 6 introduced you to some of the preparatory stages and planning that you need to undertake when approaching an assignment. This chapter begins to introduce various approaches and strategies that can assist you in organising an assignment in order to get going and actually produce written work.

Structuring assignments

Chapter 9 looks into different kinds of assignments in greater detail, but regardless of whether your assignment is an essay, report or project, some common features of writing at an academic level remain the same. This is particularly true with regard to the way in which you go about structuring a piece of written work.

It won't come as any surprise to you that the overall structure of just about any assignment will need to reflect the following three parts:

INTRODUCTION
What are you going to do?
Why and How?

MAIN BODY
Do it!
Present and explore your main areas for discussion, accompanied with supporting evidence

CONCLUSION
Remind the reader what you've done and emphasise your final judgement or point(s)

The sandwich model

This chapter will look into each of these parts in more detail shortly, but to begin with a useful way to consider the component parts of an assignment might be with the sandwich model, which illustrates helpful points about the balance of various parts of an assignment, and all the component parts required (Figure 8.1).

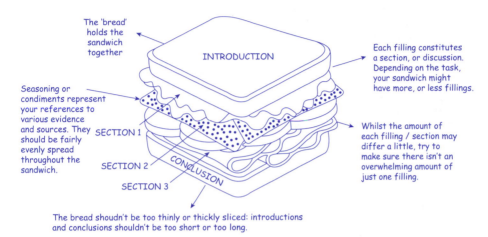

The 'bread' holds the sandwich together

Each filling constitutes a section, or discussion. Depending on the task, your sandwich might have more, or less fillings.

Seasoning or condiments represent your references to various evidence and sources. They should be fairly evenly spread throughout the sandwich.

Whilst the amount of each filling / section may differ a little, try to make sure there isn't an overwhelming amount of just one filling.

INTRODUCTION

SECTION 1

SECTION 2

SECTION 3

CONCLUSION

The bread shouldn't be too thinly or thickly sliced: introductions and conclusions shouldn't be too short or too long.

Figure 8.1   The sandwich assignment model

Although every sandwich is slightly different, Figure 8.1 shows how an assignment can be thought of in this way to help keep it balanced, and to include all the necessary component parts. Consider yourself eating the sandwich: you wouldn't want a bite that was made up predominantly of disproportionally thick bread, and you wouldn't want a mouthful of all the condiments (e.g. a sauce or relish) on one occasion, but none on another. Keeping this image in mind, of a well-balanced sandwich with all the necessary parts, can help you to keep focused upon the structure of an assignment.

Characteristics of strong introductions

The introduction to an assignment is crucial, so don't think this is something you can avoid or skip over, although it is worth pointing out that oftentimes an introduction is something that the writer will return to *after* completing the assignment, to polish up or make changes if the assignment has changed significantly during the writing process.

There are several purposes to an introduction:

- To give the reader a broad indication of what (i.e. the subject area) the work is concerned with.
- To explain what the work is going to do and how it will go about this (what it will cover and perhaps some indication as to the structure).

It may also be an appropriate place to exhibit some of your critical thinking and analysis skills by:

- Providing some rationale or justification for the focus in a piece of writing (Why is this an issue worth investigating?)
- Explaining/defining or 'unpacking' any key terms or concepts that may be central to the work.

This will depend on the length and nature of the piece of work and any particular guidance you have been given by your tutors.

Another model that can be helpful to consider when thinking about the level of *depth and detail* in an Introduction is to consider a shape similar to that of a traditional egg timer, or hourglass shape (Figure 8.2).

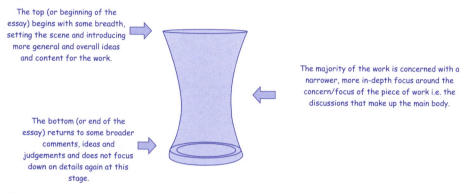

The top (or beginning of the essay) begins with some breadth, setting the scene and introducing more general and overall ideas and content for the work.

The majority of the work is concerned with a narrower, more in-depth focus around the concern/focus of the piece of work i.e. the discussions that make up the main body.

The bottom (or end of the essay) returns to some broader comments, ideas and judgements and does not focus down on details again at this stage.

Figure 8.2   An hourglass visualisation of an assignment

This hourglass model, then, reiterates that the introduction is not a place for many details or to launch into your discussions in-depth. It is where you begin with breadth and equip the reader with the things they need to know in order to navigate and understand the rest of the work. Beware of spending *too* long on your introduction – it has a job to do, but should not give too much away; make sure the reader still wants to go on to read the rest of your work! Also, it should not take up a disproportionate amount of the word allocation for the essay. For example, if you were writing a 2,000-word essay, then proportionally, you might loosely allocate your word count as *approximately*:

Introduction: 300–400 words
Main body: 1,200 words, split into 4 issues, or sections
Conclusion: 300–400 words

However, resist the temptation of becoming too tied up with word counts for each section, as they can be very restrictive and sometimes prevent you from producing good writing. Have a loose word count in mind but don't become a martyr to this; as you'll see later in this chapter, part of the drafting and rewriting process includes editing, where you will no doubt have to make some tough decisions about deleting some of your writing to adhere to a word count.

Comparing introductions

Below are two short introductions for the same assignment. Both have strengths and weaknesses. Try to directly compare them and identify characteristics of each that you feel are good and characteristics that you feel are not particularly useful.

Essay title: Critically discuss the range of influences upon the development of key education policies from the Second World War to the 1997 New Labour government, with reference to significant legislation and influential theories of the time.

Introduction 1	Introduction 2
This essay is concerned with examining English educational policy during the post-war period up until the late 1990s, which was a very important era where many changes were made. At this time, many changes had occurred in the country and there was hope for particular changes to create more educational opportunities and develop a system of education that could be tailored to each kind of pupil.	There were many influences on the way that the education system developed in the time following World War Two, with significant changes very much dependent upon which political party was in government at the time.
	After an exploration of the tri-partite system originating in the 1940s, there will be a particular focus upon Conservative education policies in the 1980s, a period of time when Margaret Thatcher was prime minister.
This assignment is going to look into the reasons for these changes with reference to significant legislation which will be explored in chronological order: the 1944 Education Act, Circular 10/65, and the 1988 Education Reform Act in particular.	The policies will be assessed by looking at different aspects and making reference to different sources that support or contrast ideas.

Neither example is 'perfect' and both have room for improvement. Characteristics of them you may have observed in each include:

- **In Introduction 1:** Somewhat vague language is used, that is, 'a very important era where many changes were made' and then repetition of this in the subsequent line. Although an introduction should not start talking about points in too much detail, the use of the word 'important' here is somewhat elusive. Also, try to avoid repeating the same word several times in just a few sentences – 'changes' is used four times here. However, it may be helpful to the reader to know what pieces of legislation will be focused upon, and the fact that the writer has said they will be explored in chronological order also 'signposts' what is coming in the work, and the order of it, which is a good habit to establish.

- **In Introduction 2:** A slightly more specific opening statement that acknowledges a range of influences and draws attention in particular to the significance of political parties. Again, there is some 'signposting' by telling the reader what the work will cover, although the reader may be slightly concerned that there will be a big jump from the 1940s to the 1980s. It's also not necessary to drop in one such specific detail (i.e. that Margaret Thatcher was prime minister), as this isn't a helpful or necessary piece of information needed here. Lastly, the final sentence about what the work will do is not a particularly good use of words; anyone reading the work would naturally expect the writer to be looking at varying perspectives on an issue and to refer to literature to support the claims, so explaining this is verging on stating the obvious.

Consider the following in crafting your introduction:

1   What broad issue(s) or agenda is the work concerned with?

2   Why is this important? Or, why is it an issue worthy of exploration?

3   What key sections or discussions will therefore be necessary to cover?

4   What can the reader expect?

Using this guidance, a simple but effective introduction to the essay question posed above might be:

> From the post-war period of 1945 to the election of New Labour in 1997, the English education system underwent many far-reaching alterations, and these have resulted in complex changes in policy and provision for parents, teachers and pupils. This essay is going to examine some of the reasons for changes in policy during these decades, drawing on significant legislation, policy and theoretical ideas that all shaped the changes.
>
> Initially the work will provide an overview of these changes, moving on to focus on three particularly significant policy changes in-depth: the tri-partite system; the introduction of comprehensive schooling; and the creation of a schools market. As each of these policies is examined, discussion will take into account the range of social, political, economic and educational pressures that all contributed to the development of the policies, and subsequently the impact of their implementation.

Organising the main body

The main body of an assignment is comprised of a series of discussions, sections or considerations of particular issues or themes. The actual composition of the main body will depend upon the nature of the assignment you've been given and the way in which you are going to be structuring the work. Each section of the main body is an opportunity to demonstrate your knowledge and understanding of that particular issue, and to make sure that what you present is directly contributing to answering the question or task set.

There are a number of different ways that you might organise the main body of your work, such as chronologically or according to key theories. Ideally each section should address and work through one particular coherent and fairly discrete issue or theme. So for example, taking the essay question explored in Activity 8.1 when considering Introductions, two different ways to structure this assignment might be:

Structure 1	Structure 2
Introduction	Introduction
Background information	Background information
1944 Act	Economic influences from 1944 to 1997
Circular 10/65	Social influences from 1944 to 1997
Education Reform Act 1988	Political influences from 1944 to 1997
Conclusion	Conclusion

The first outline, based on a chronological structure, is straightforward to organise and plan. Each time period is kept in its own discrete section of the work, and discussion and analysis of each of these occurs in that part. The risk with this structure is that it can be easy to slip into a descriptive story about each policy.

The second structure identifies key themes that run throughout all time periods. So, this would be more challenging to plan, but would be more likely to result in a deeper level of critical analysis and comparison about the impact of these influences across a time period.

One approach to *avoid* is presenting a ream of information in a 'shopping list'-style approach. If the writer simply lists points, perspectives, pieces of legislation or studies then these are pieces of information that are being considered in isolation which does not facilitate analysis or discussion. A good example of this is covered in the next chapter in the focus upon literature reviews as a type of assignment.

Each section (or sandwich filling) needs to:

- Present the issue for consideration and show knowledge of the issue.
- Demonstrate your awareness and understanding of different perspectives on the issue.
- Supply evidence for the claims you're making in the form of references to relevant literature.
- Incorporate critical thinking and display logic, criticality of thought and efforts towards making judgements upon the issues under consideration in that section.

Each section is likely to be comprised of several paragraphs, and so letting the reader know when each section is beginning and closing is of particular importance. This is where the kind of language you use is significant; clear and concise guidance for the reader about what the work is doing, and the direction it is going in can make a big difference.

Signposting and language

One very effective way to demonstrate your logic, planning, linking of ideas and progression in the work is through the kind of language you use to guide and inform the reader as to what you are doing. This not only ensures that the reader knows where the work is going and why, but also helps you, the writer, to be certain about your purpose and progression. Therefore, the use of linking, signposting and transition words and phrases is an important skill to work on developing, so that you have plenty of these expressions at your disposal.

Consider the following example:

> **As highlighted previously**, a particularly significant influence upon the emergence of comprehensive schools was related to criticisms of the tri-partite system and **therefore it is pertinent to identify and explore** some of these. **In this next section**, some viewpoints from prominent commentators in the 1950s and 1960s **will be presented**, **but before this**, it is important to understand the origins of the tri-partite system, **an overview of which follows**.

The words in bold are all examples of words or phrases that are used to, essentially, tell the reader what the work is doing and why.

Can you draw up a list of other words that would effectively link paragraphs, indicate transitions from one discussion to another or assist the reader to understand the purpose and direction of the work? A few more examples are provided here to begin:

- To surmise ...
- However, it should be noted that ...
- Also of significance at this time was ...
- Another influential theory was that of ...

The University of Manchester has an excellent resource called the Academic Phrasebank which has a wealth of phrases you can use to help convey your intentions in academic work, such as how to introduce examples, present comparisons and explain causes and consequences – see www.phrasebank.manchester.ac.uk/.

Creating synthesis and an evidence-based conclusion

Conclusions are a part of academic work that students consistently find challenging. It is quite a task to sum up and reflect back upon potentially several thousand words containing important ideas, theories and viewpoints into a paragraph or two to leave the reader with your final judgements and impress upon them your knowledge and understanding.

Firstly, it can be helpful to realise what is *not* useful in a conclusion. There are a few key points here to bear in mind:

- Don't repeat what you've written in the work; re-presenting specific ideas, details or pieces of information does not help to create a synthesis.
- Avoid too much detail or introducing any new ideas or content; if you think of something that you feel is particularly important and deserves exploration in the essay then you need to find a home for it in the main body.
- Don't make it too long …

An effective conclusion should:

- Make it clear how the work has 'answered' the essay question or responded well to the task set.
- Present some kind of judgement or concluding ideas (even if these remain somewhat neutral rather than a definitive Yes/No response).
- Try to synthesise the many details you may have put in the work into a few broader, overall points.

Imagine that someone has asked you to report to them three or four *overall* ideas or points you've learned as a result of undertaking the work for that assignment; this is a good starting point. Be sure to also use words and phrases that make it explicitly clear to the reader what you've done and how this has contributed to meeting the requirements of the task you've been set.

Note in the example below comments about the issues the work has covered (a summary), the significance of what has been highlighted (why it matters) and comments that offer up some kind of judgement on the issues under consideration. Remember that making a 'judgement' about something doesn't mean you are coming down in agreement (or disagreement) with a particular point of view. It simply means that as a result of what you have considered in your discussions (i.e. you need to be able to have shown the evidence for your judgement by way of what you've analysed in the work), you are able to present some kind of final points that you feel are a good 'answer' to the question. Sometimes, this means sitting on the fence after demonstrating both sides of an argument, or acknowledging that an issue is complex and cannot be easily summed up with a particular decision.

Example conclusion

This work has illustrated the vast changes undergone within the education system during the latter half of the twentieth century, highlighting in particular the impact of shifting ideals and priorities in politics, society, and the economy.

Discussions have illustrated how different viewpoints around children's capabilities and destinies were of significant impact and resulted in far-reaching disparities in educational achievement and opportunity. Of particular note has been the consistent theme of prospects for many learners being dependent upon social class and the ways in which education can be both a barrier and a facilitator for social mobility. The emergence in the latter half of this time period of the concepts of parental choice and a schools market has also been recognised as transformational, marking the beginning of the complex and often controversial variety which continues in the present-day schools system in this country.

Broken down into the component parts:

This work has illustrated the vast changes undergone within the education system during the latter half of the twentieth century, highlighting in particular the impact of shifting ideals and priorities in politics, society, and the economy	A broad overview of what the work has done and some of the general themes that have been identified as significant in the work
Discussions have illustrated how different viewpoints around children's capabilities and destinies were of significant impact and resulted in far-reaching disparities in educational achievement and opportunity	Key finding/conclusion 1
Of particular note has been the consistent theme of prospects for many learners being dependent upon social class and the ways in which education can be both a barrier and a facilitator for social mobility	Key finding/conclusion 2
The emergence in the latter half of this time period of the concepts of parental choice and a schools market has also been recognised as transformational, marking the beginning of the complex and often controversial variety which continues in the present-day schools system in this country	Key finding/conclusion 3 And A forward-looking final comment that shows understanding of both past and present policy

Be sure to note the style, tone, depth and scope of comments you come across in your own reading, looking at the nature of conclusions in book chapters, journal articles and other resources you may draw upon.

Drafting and writing

After deciding what you'd like to say, you're now at the point where you can say it, well write it – you can start to compose your points into a draft. Often just committing ideas to paper, regardless of the quality of these, is a must, and planning and drafting will make the whole writing process easier later on.

Knowing what you'd like to say (or argue)

As we mentioned earlier in this chapter, there are a number of ways you can organise the points that make up the main body of your assignment. You may wish to present the information you've collected, for example different theories and research studies, chronologically or thematically. It will very much depend on the task that you've been asked to complete. Writing a draft is joining up this information together, connecting one point to another and so on. You will draft your writing to connect your notes, for example about a theorist, with the findings from a piece of research by another author or perhaps two studies which support the argument you're making. It may be messy at first but the planning and drafting process will help you with the writing process later on. If we go back to the sandwich model we highlighted earlier in this chapter, it will help you to make sure your bread isn't too thick and your condiments are spread evenly throughout your sandwich.

You should avoid presenting a ream of information in a 'shopping list'-style. Although your reader (and marker) is interested in the information you've researched and the facts you're presenting, they are also interested in the ways in which you present this and how you demonstrate your knowledge and understanding. They want to see evidence that you have evaluated different perspectives and critically analysed pieces of legislation and the findings of different studies. So you need to think about how you are going to organise the information in your draft. One way to do this is to colour code the information and notes that you have. For example, assign a colour for each section of your assignment. The notes you have made on your research and the supporting quotations about one perspective could be blue, and those that you have made about another one could be yellow. This technique is useful because it can help you to visualise the structure of your ideas and arguments.

When you are organising your draft, and building up your sections and arguments, headings and subheadings may also be useful. These will help you to give a sense of structure to your draft and this can help you to see where your argument is developing. It is, however, important to keep an open mind at this stage in the drafting process, as your sections could develop and change so it's best not to have any headings or subheadings set in stone. You can be flexible with your writing right up until you have a final draft. While you are composing the draft another tip is to write a summary of the key ideas presented in each of the sections so that you have a list of the main points that you can draw upon when you write your conclusion.

Paragraph construction, linking and signposting

Look carefully at journal articles you come across in your reading and research. Do you notice any patterns when it comes to the structuring of the paragraphs? Within academic texts there are often noticeable patterns in the way they are constructed or written. The paragraphs begin with a topic sentence. This sentence tells the reader about the focus and purpose of the paragraph. The other sentences then develop the ideas from this sentence further and contribute to the construction of the argument being made. At the end of the paragraph a sentence then closes the paragraph. This sentence can take a number of different formats and helps the writer to signal to the reader what the next steps are. For example, the sentence may conclude the ideas being discussed or it may link to the paragraph which follows it. PEEL – Point, Explanation, Evidence/Examples and Link – is a helpful tip that is often learnt in schools and can also be used for writing at university. Once you've stated the topic sentence and illustrated the purpose of the paragraph, the supporting explanation can help to clarify the ideas, and evidence from relevant literature or examples from educational practice help to illustrate these before the final sentence in the paragraph links to the next one.

The linking of paragraphs is very important because it signals to the reader that the information you're presenting is helping to build your argument. To link the paragraphs effectively you need to draw on signposting words. As we discussed earlier in the chapter, these are words that help to signal transitions between sentences (and paragraphs) and illustrate to the reader what the work is doing. Think carefully about the choice of signposting words that you use because if they do not make sense the direction of your transitions and consequently your argument(s) can become confusing.

Moving from the broad to the specific: avoiding generalisations, using precise but not overcomplex language

When drafting a piece of work another factor to think about is moving from the broad context about a topic to the specific details. As discussed earlier in this chapter and illustrated in Figure 8.2 (the hourglass image), the beginning of an assignment, the introduction, should set the scene for the rest of the piece of writing. You should introduce the topic by outlining some of the more general ideas – for example, what the topic is, whether it has been extensively explored, and who by, for instance, researchers, practitioners and policy-makers. Once you have established the setting you will need to narrow down your focus and begin to present and discuss more specific information that is relevant to your topic and argument. You should give some detailed information on the specific topic you're focusing on before giving more in-depth and focused attention to the topic in the main body of your assignment. To do this you need to have an understanding of the key concepts and terminology that are relevant to the topic. A good tip, particularly if you're learning a new topic area with concepts that are difficult to grasp, is to keep a vocabulary book (or list if using a computer). When you come across unfamiliar words and terms in lectures and seminars or in your independent reading and research you can make a note of them and look up their meanings and the contexts in which they can be used. However, it is important that the language you use is not overcomplex. It is better to use language that you understand effectively than to try and include terminology that you may have misunderstood. Your writing will demonstrate understanding which is more rewarding than just using misunderstood words.

Using references and supporting evidence to add value rather than a tick box exercise

If we had a pound for every time we are asked 'How many references do I need to include?' we would probably be quite wealthy by now! There is no golden rule regarding the number of references required in an essay – there should be as many references as you need to support your viewpoints. References or citations in your text help you to demonstrate knowledge and understanding as they substantiate your viewpoint, support your ideas. Supporting your ideas is an essential part of constructing an argument. In addition to this, referencing also illustrates to your reader/marker that you have read around your topic and that you have an ability to paraphrase text. As we highlighted in Chapter 4, effective paraphrasing demonstrates more understanding than just copying and directly quoting some text. Rather than thinking 'Have I got enough references?' you should ask yourself 'Are all of my points supported with evidence from the literature?'.

As the research and literature cited within assignments are a part of the writing, they should be carefully written into sentences and introduced by the writer rather than just placed into a sentence or left hanging on the page with no careful consideration. Consider these two examples:

Adolescent friendships might be associated with identity development, because it encompasses the acceptance within the friendship of the individual as an autonomous, independent individual who has own ideas and needs (Doeselaar, Meeus, Koot and Branje, 2016, p. 29).

As Doeselaar, Meeus, Koot and Branje (2016, p. 29) suggest, the balanced relatedness 'aspect of Adolescent friendships might be associated with identity development, because it encompasses the acceptance within the friendship of the individual as an autonomous, independent individual who has own ideas and needs'. (quotation taken from van Doeselaar, L., Meeus, W., Koot, H.M. and Branje, S. (2016) 'The role of best friends in educational identity formation in adolescence', *Journal of Adolescence,* Vol. 47, pp. 28–37).

As you can see, the second example does not disrupt the flow of the academic writing and adds value to the sentence.

ACTIVITY 8.3

Inserting references

The in-text references have been removed from this extract. Insert the references where you think they should be.

> *Success in higher education is inextricably entwined with learning and knowledge construction demonstrated in academic writing as the medium for summative assessment is usually written. Against the backdrop of the expansion of higher education and diversification of the student population increasing demands are being placed on lecturers and specialists such as writing tutors to ensure students meet the standards of writing demanded in Higher Education (HE). This is exacerbated by the perceived tension that students cannot write at a university standard as they are insufficiently prepared for such demands. Therefore, it is essential to ask questions about how we can ensure that all students can meet the demands of HE.*

See the end of the chapter for answers.

Final checks

Once you have written your draft you need to proofread and edit it before then making any final checks. As we pointed out in Chapter 6, it is important to give yourself time between the edits and final checks so that you have some distance between yourself as a writer and yourself as an editor. This will help you to spot if you need a reference to support your viewpoint or where your writing may be descriptive and 'waffley' rather than critical and analytical. As well as checking the referencing, structure and spelling, punctuation and grammar, you should also make sure the information required for submission and formatting is correct. Every university will have different requirements so check with your lecturers what is required in terms of student ID number, page numbers, the positioning of the title (e.g. left spaced or centralised) and so on.

TIP

To help with making the final checks:

- Read aloud – this will help you to focus on the words and the flow of your writing.
- Read your assignment backwards (sentence by sentence) – similarly to reading aloud, starting with the very last sentence and reading your assignment backwards will help you to focus on the words; you need to question whether they are the correct words. Do they help you to convey meaning?
- Ask a friend or relative to read your work – they may not understand the topic, but they can still tell you if the writing makes sense.

Chapter summary: useful points for you to implement

- Organising an assignment and knowing about the characteristics of each part is key.
- Try to balance out the content of your work by thinking about the breadth, depth, length and balance in your work.
- Don't neglect the introduction or conclusion to a piece of work which can be crucial.
- Make sure you use connectives and signposting in your writing to help guide your reader.
- Consider where to place your in-text references so that they do not disrupt the flow of sentences.
- Drafting is an important part of the writing process and you should leave plenty of time for the task – writing always takes longer than you think!

Answers to Activity 8.3

Inserting references:

> Success in higher education is inextricably entwined with learning and knowledge construction demonstrated in academic writing **(Sommerville and Crème, 2005)** as the medium for summative assessment is usually written **(Lea, 1999)**. Against the backdrop of the expansion of higher education and diversification of the student population **(Ashwin, 2006)** increasing demands are being placed on lecturers and specialists such as writing tutors to ensure students meet the standards of writing demanded in Higher Education (HE). This is exacerbated by the perceived tension that students cannot write at a university standard as they are insufficiently prepared for such demands **(Lowe & Cook, 2003)**. Therefore, it is essential to ask questions about how we can ensure that all students can meet the demands of HE.

Different Kinds of Written Assignments

Within your Education programme, you are likely to encounter a variety of different kinds of assignments or assessed work. Your programme will have been designed in this way to enable you to gain skills and experience of writing in different kinds of ways for different audiences, and ultimately to prepare you for tasks you may need to undertake in further study or future employment.

The kinds of assessed work you might be asked to produce could include: essays (some of these may be reflective in nature); reports; journals/diaries; oral presentations; poster presentations; projects; reports of primary data collection and analysis; literature reviews; critical reviews; annotated bibliographies; lesson plans; or teaching resources.

This chapter covers the most common assessment types used in Education programmes and provides you with in-depth clarification and advice on producing:

- Essays.
- Reports.
- Literature reviews.
- More substantial pieces of work such as dissertations or final-year projects.

Essays

Writing an essay is synonymous with studying many subjects at university. Although you're unlikely to progress into a job where you write essays on a day-to-day basis, the fact is you probably won't be able to get away from them on your Education course.

It is useful to recognise that essays are not a perfect form of assessment: a whole range of criticisms are levelled at essays as an assessment method, but undergoing the task of writing an essay is also a very constructive experience. Whether you're a fan or not, learning how to write an effective essay is essential. Through preparing and writing an essay you will illustrate to your tutors:

- Your ability to research, select and utilise relevant information.
- Your ability to reason, pursue an argument and weigh up a range of perspectives.
- Your commitment to research and reading.

Champions of the essay say …	Opponents of the essay say …
– They are a really useful tool to use for students to receive individualised feedback about their thoughts and understanding on an issue	– They can be easy for students to plagiarise
– They are a good test of communication skills	– They're an outdated way to assess
– They require a range of skills to be used from start to finish	– Not all students are strong at conveying their understanding in a formal, written manner

An essay …

- Is a response to some kind of provocative question or task that requires consideration of a range of different viewpoints and pieces of evidence.
- Identifies concluding points that have been arrived at as a result of evidence-based judgements made on the material, ideas and theories that have been examined.
- Demands analysis, evaluation and critique of various perspectives.
- Does not usually use subheadings or bullet points, but introduces new discussions and portions of the work through a logical structure and linkages using signposting language.
- Usually presents evidence in the form of words rather than images, graphs or tables.
- Has a clear structure comprised of an introduction, main body and conclusion (see Chapter 6).

In all pieces of academic work, but particularly in essays, it is useful to bear in mind a model of educational development or educational goals that was originally developed by Benjamin Bloom in 1956 – it's likely you will come across this model in your studies. The model has been developed, revised and remains subject to ongoing critical analysis (as should occur with all educational ideas), but the original model (Figure 9.1) is helpful to illustrate the kinds of progression you should be aiming for in your work.

The model illustrates how a certain order of skills (working from the bottom up) can be developed in order to help learners aspire to more complex levels of thinking. In terms of students in higher education, it's quite a commonly used approach to think of learners scaling the levels, from displaying their ability to remember information early in their studies to moving all the way up to making informed judgements and appraisals – although developments of this model have altered the highest level to 'Create', a function thought to demand more complex and challenging mental skill and function (see http://thesecondprinciple.com/teaching-essentials/beyond-bloom-cognitive-taxonomy-revised/).

With regard to essay writing, then, in a simplistic sense bear in mind that in your undergraduate Education studies if your work remains at the lower levels of the pyramid during your time as a student, you will find achieving higher marks much

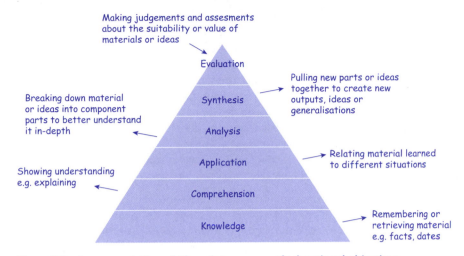

Figure 9.1   A representation of Bloom's taxonomy of educational objectives

more challenging. To plan, develop draft and refine a strong essay you should use the guidance in this book provided in Chapters 6, 7 and 8, all of which is relevant to a range of written assignments, but predominantly designed to support you with essay writing.

The remainder of this chapter now moves to examine a range of other written assignments you may come across in your studies.

Reports

It's important to consider here the difference between an essay and a report, as the two have some commonalities and differences. Compared to the characteristics of an essay (as outlined in the previous section), a report has a different kind of purpose and format that you need to take into account when approaching an assignment that requires you to write a report.

A report …

- Is often a write-up of some kind of 'research' you have undertaken, often primary research where you have gathered empirical data, analysed this and then present the findings. They may include graphs, diagrams or tables.
- Reports tend to make recommendations at the end – suggestions based on the evidence that has been examined and the conclusions arrived at.
- Reports tend to be more descriptive than an essay, with less analysis and critical discussion. They are more of a straightforward write-up of events or findings, and are often (but not always) shorter than an essay.
- Reports usually have a fixed structure and present information using a number of different sections, or headings and subheadings. They often break information up using bullet points, which are generally not used in essays.

Depending upon the brief you have been given, the task behind your report may be to write up the findings of a small-scale piece of research you have conducted, to report upon an experience you have had such as a field trip, to 'test' a solution or hypothesis with regard to a particular issue, or to provide a narrative to report upon another piece of work you have undertaken – for example, a report to accompany a group work project, or rationale report for a lesson plan you may have prepared.

In many ways, a report still necessitates the same components as an essay: you need to undertake extensive research and reading to gather the knowledge required, such as existing data and theories that are relevant to that particular area, or if you have gathered empirical data you will need to be able to write about what you did, and why you went about it in that particular way.

Although this may differ slightly depending on the guidance you have been given, generally the key components (or main sections) required in a report are:

Title: This should be a clear description of the content and purpose of the report, in just one sentence or statement. It may be on its own cover page for the document, check if there are any specific formatting or submission requirements in this respect.

Abstract: This is a brief overview or summary of the work. It should describe the focus of the work, what has been done and the key findings. Therefore, this needs to be written last, as you won't know what your findings are until you have completed the work! Abstracts are usually very concise, of around 150–200 words.

Introduction: Here you need to introduce the reader to the broad topic or issue(s) the work is concerned with, and give some rationale for this focus. This is also a suitable place to introduce any particular terminology or equip the reader with any background knowledge they may need in order to understand or better navigate the report. You should make the aim(s) of the work clear and sometimes you may need to identify specific objectives, that is what you intend to achieve, or what the outcome should be.

Literature review: As the name suggests, this is where you need to provide a succinct review of what is already known in this area, identifying and summarising the key points of the most prominent or significant existing studies, theories or ideas in this area. The purpose of this section is to give further context for your work and to also demonstrate where your contribution (i.e. the report, although unpublished to the wider world) fits into what is already known about this area – for example, there might be a lack of very recent studies, your purpose or hypothesis might be contrary to what already exists in the literature, or there may have been new and significant policy changes that could impact upon the issue under consideration. This section will need to feature (and reference correctly) a wide range of relevant sources to support and substantiate the claims you're making. See further on in this chapter for more detailed guidance about approaching and planning literature reviews.

Methodology: If you are reporting on a piece of empirical research (see Chapter 1) then you will need to clearly explain what you have done and how. That is, you will need to describe what kinds of data you have gathered, from whom and how you analysed this. If your research is based on secondary data (see Chapter 1) then you will need to explain what sort of sources you accessed, or what kind of tools or terms you used to effectively search existing literature. If your research is gathering primary data, then you will need to go into more depth and talk about access to and characteristics of your sample, the research tools used (e.g. questionnaire), ethical precautions, the actual procedure (i.e. what you did) and how you analysed the data. For more information on writing about research methodologies, see the section later in this chapter which expands upon this in relation to dissertations.

Findings: Here you will present the output after analysing the data you have gathered. Depending on the kind of data you have gathered, you may be presenting statistics, tables, graphs, images, or passages of text. The data you include needs to be organised and presented in a systematic way and at an appropriate level of detail depending on the word count you have been given for the report. If it's a fairly lengthy piece of work, then it's useful to summarise the key findings at the end of this section.

Discussion: In this part of the report you need to consider your findings and relate them back to key points from the literature review. The main aim here is to establish where your findings fit in with what is already known about the area – for example, does what you have found consolidate and reflect what you found in the literature? Or are your findings contrary to prominent ideas? Perhaps your findings simply contribute a different perspective?

Conclusion/recommendations: These may or may not be separate sections in your report, depending on the length and depth required. A conclusion needs to draw all the strands together and identify what the key messages are to be taken away as a result of the investigation. It needs to return to the objectives or hypotheses you established at the beginning (in the introduction) and consider to what extent these have been met or proved/disproved. If you are required to present recommendations, then these should be systematic and specific. It should be clear where the evidence in your report has come from to support the recommendation (cross-reference them) and it is best to number them so they are presented clearly and succinctly.

References: Provide a list of all sources you have referred to in the work, presented using the appropriate referencing convention (usually Harvard).

Appendices: Check as to whether these are required or permitted; it is dependent on the purpose of the report and bear in mind that sometimes these may still be included in your word count, so it's important to check with your tutor on this matter. Appendices for a report might typically include examples of data collection tools you used (e.g. the questionnaire you gave to participants) or supplementary data (such as an example of a transcript you analysed, evidence of ethical approval or access from a setting).

Literature reviews

A literature review is usually the kind of task required as learners progress in their studies, commonly as part of a dissertation or as an assignment task in itself. A literature review task is sometimes initially confused with a 'critical review' but the key difference here is that a critical review is usually an in-depth analysis of just *one* piece of work, whereas a literature review considers *many* pieces of work. That might sound a little daunting, but it is an excellent way to allow you to illustrate how much reading and research you have completed in an area, and your subsequent understanding of this.

A literature review ...

- Should represent a wide range of reading, usually across different kinds of sources, that is, books, journal articles, reports.
- Will seek to take an analytical approach to the literature and include critical comments upon trends and characteristics of the literature.
- Is a thorough, critical and reflective account of what has been written by researchers, theorists or writers in that area.

The best way to gain an understanding of what a literature review looks and sounds like is to consider a few different examples.

The first excerpt is from a literature review about the experiences of refugee and asylum seeking children in the UK, published in 2005. One chapter of this review looks at educational experiences of children who are new to the UK, and Activity 9.1 is just one paragraph from that chapter.

ACTIVITY 9.1

Identifying characteristics of a literature review 1

Read the collection of excerpts below then consider the questions posed afterwards:

It is clear that in order to do well in UK schools the support that refugee children need goes beyond the curriculum. There is a great deal of writing around the cultural bias of education and how this disadvantages students from black and minority ethnic backgrounds (Ahmed, 2004).

Hamilton, Daly and Fiddy (2003) highlight this in their study and go on to point out that this was despite the fact that the government had announced that refugee and asylum seeking children could specifically be discounted in relation to performance tables. Other studies across the UK (GLA, 2004; John et al, 2002; Marriott, 2001; Stanley, 2001) concur with these findings.

Many young refugees talk about the importance of learning English and how this is a crucial factor in helping them to settle in school, in terms of education and social relationships (Candappa, 2000). Other studies (Marriott, 2001; Stanley, 2001) confirm this with as many as 82% of young people saying that learning English was the most important thing for them on arrival. The importance of both refugee support and language support teachers has been consistently highlighted as being crucial to this (Rutter & Jones, 1998; Rutter, 2003a).

Source: Hek, R. (2005) *The Experiences and Needs of Refugee and Asylum Seeking Children in the UK: A Literature Review*. Retrieved from http://dera.ioe.ac.uk/5398/1/RR635.pdf Last accessed 5th May 2018

Question

What do you note about the writing style and use of sources in this excerpt?

You may have noticed several features of the Hek excerpt that are slightly different to other assignment tasks you have completed before. For example, that:

- There is a lot of **citation of multiple sources** – that is, listing lots of sources together to support just one claim. This adds additional weight to a claim and demonstrates how extensive your reading has been.
- It **makes explicit reference to the literature** – for example 'There is a great deal of writing around the cultural bias'; 'various studies'; 'other studies'.
- There are lots of efforts to highlight the fact that **various findings have been established by different pieces of research** – for example, 'Other studies concur with these findings'; 'Other studies confirm this'; 'The importance of ... has been consistently highlighted'.
- **Every point made stems from the literature** – that is, Hek doesn't say something then add literature; she takes the literature as her starting point – she doesn't present a point to the reader unless it has feature in existing literature.
- Hek cites some of **the same authors** more than once but she **cites different pieces of their work** (i.e. from different years). This is an indication not only that Hek is very aware of what's in the field, but also that the authors she is mentioning must be well known and prominent in this area because they have clearly written a lot on the subject.

So, it should be apparent that the emphasis really is upon the 'literature' in a literature review.

Another short excerpt can help to illustrate some more characteristics. The paragraph in Activity 9.2 is taken from a report about the educational experiences of young people with caring responsibilities.

ACTIVITY 9.2

Identifying characteristics of a literature review 2

Read through this and then try to identify particularly notable characteristics again:

> Early research into young caring was, of necessity, small scale. This was because as young caring began to emerge as a social issue, young carers were hidden: there were no support services available to them until the early 1990s and these were initially small pilot projects set up in the north of England. Thus, while some early studies did identify young people who had missed school and experienced educational difficulties as a result of their caring roles (Aldridge and Becker, 1993; Frank, 1995), others did not (Bilsborrow, 1992). However, as the number of young carers projects began to grow, anecdotal evidence from project staff suggested that many young carers were experiencing educational problems. An evaluation of three of the first young carers projects to be developed showed educational difficulties to be widespread (Mahon and Higgins, 1995).

Source: Dearden, C. and Becker, S. (2002) *Young Carers and Education*. Retrieved from: http://ycrg.org.uk/youngCarersDownload/yceduc%5B1%5D.pdf Last accessed on 12 December 2015.

In this excerpt, you may note that there is a more **analytical treatment of the literature**. Examples of this are:

- Comment upon the **emergence of research in the area** – 'Early research into young caring was, of necessity, small scale. This was because as young caring began to emerge as a social issue, young carers were hidden.'
- Critical comment about **the scope of studies** – 'while some early studies did identify young people who had missed school ... others did not.'
- Acknowledgement that **the focus of research** has changed – 'As it has become apparent that many young carers have educational problems, research has sought to establish ...'
- It identifies **gaps in the research** – 'No other research has looked at variables that may have an impact on young carers' educational disadvantage.'

Other examples that you might wish to look at are:

Peters, S. (2010) *Literature Review: Transition from Early Childhood Education to School*. Retrieved from: http://ece.manukau.ac.nz/__data/assets/pdf_file/0008/85841/956_ECELitReview.pdf Last accessed on 5 May 2018.

Novelli, M., Higgins, S., Ugur, M. and Valiente, O. (2014) *The Political Economy of Education Systems in Conflict-Affected Areas*. Retrieved from: www.gov.uk/government/uploads/system/uploads/attachment_data/file/469101/political-economy-conflict-affected.pdf Last accessed on 5 May 2018.

Warning! These are very lengthy reviews, commissioned for the purpose of informing policy makers, not for the purposes of a university assignment; however, just a scan through these reviews reveals their emphasis upon being thorough, informative and extensively well researched (Figure 9.2).

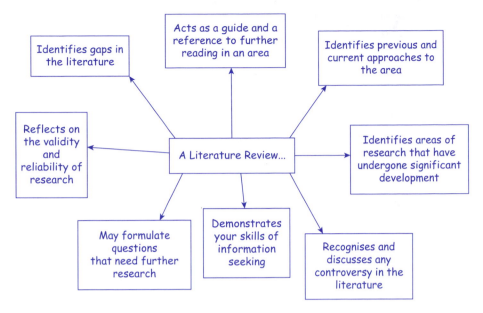

Figure 9.2   An overview of the purpose of a literature review

Planning a literature review

As you might imagine, being prepared to write a literature review involves a great deal of reading. The crucial approach to take here is to make sure that you are organised in the way you search, save and record the kinds of literature you are using. You might find it helpful to refer back to Chapter 2 here to remind you of some pointers and research and reading techniques.

On some occasions you may be asked to write a literature review on a topic given to you, on others you might be given free rein to select a topic based on your own interest. Regardless, most students begin with quite a broad area of interest, and have to undergo the process of broadly reviewing their area of interest, and then narrowing this down. Initial ideas for a starting point might come from issues you've covered in particular modules but not had a chance to explore in depth; something you've observed while on placement in an educational setting; a controversial issue covered recently by the media; or perhaps something derived from your own school experiences.

Table 9.1 offers some examples of starting points, possible areas of focus and the kind of research question that process might end upon. Remember that any kind of research (and reviewing the literature is a kind of research) is a 'messy' business, that will at times feel a little haphazard and vast. We all begin with broad ideas and have to experience the process of narrowing these down.

It is unlikely that as an Education student you would need to conduct what is known as a 'systematic' review whereby you meticulously document how, when and where you undertook your literature search (as is common in other disciplines such

Table 9.1 Narrowing down and generating a research question

Initial topic area:	Special Educational Needs and Disabilities	Outdoor learning	Schools and child health
Related issues:	'Unseen' disabilities	School outdoor spaces	Number of obese children
At this stage a whole host of relevant issues might come to light. Consider which you're most interested in, if there is sufficient literature on these areas and the contemporary relevance of them.	Communication	Impact on social and emotional development	School meals/nutrition: messages about health
	Inclusion strategies and the impact of these	Health and Safety	Healthy Schools standard
	Recent policy changes	Space/time in curriculum	Physical Education (PE) lessons
	Funding cuts and lack of specialist support	Forest Schools development in UK	Gender differences: girls' participation
	Peer exclusion/friendship groups	Certain age groups – more common in early years?	

Once you have begun to identify a range of related issues, this is where conducting initial searches of the literature helps you to narrow down what kinds of research and publications are already available, and where there might be gaps. You can then use this initial search as a stepping stone to identify a narrower focus.

Initial topic area:	**Special Educational Needs and Disabilities**	**Outdoor learning**	**Schools and child health**
Narrowed down focus: *Choosing to focus on just one of the issues above, or perhaps combining them is a starting point here*	Communication for children on the autistic spectrum in mainstream schools	Embedding outdoor learning in the curriculum	Physical and Health education for girls in secondary schools
Your search of the literature now focuses upon issues much more specific to this narrowed down focus, using the guidance that follows in this table. The end point of a literature review if it is part of a dissertation or project that involves the collection of primary data is to generate a research question that will then guide your focus for actual data collection – for example, designing a study that would gather data from pupils in order to begin to generate possible 'answers' to your research question.			
Research question/focus:	How effective are communication strategies for children with autism spectrum disorder included in mainstream primary schools?	What are the benefits and challenges associated with greater outdoor learning in the primary school curriculum?	A critical analysis of the opportunities and experiences offered to teenage girls in PE lessons

as Health-related subjects), but it is still important to be organised in your searching for the literature you will use.

- Try to identify what kinds of **key words or terms you will use to search** for relevant literature. You might want to list these terms and then work your way through them as you use your library catalogue, databases or search engines. Some terms will produce more relevant results than others. Put plenty of time aside for your searching; it will *always* take longer than you think.
- Clarify what the expectations of the task are with regard to the **type of literature** you should access. Typically a literature review would refer to journal articles, books, government reports or statistics, and research reports from relevant organisations. Less common sources might be conference proceedings, articles in relevant periodicals, published Master's or PhD theses, policy papers or legislation.
- **Organise the sources** you will be using so that you can keep track of them. Your reading will begin to generate a number of key themes and it's really important to have some kind of system in place so that you don't get confused with all the sources you're drawing on.

Depending on the size and scope of your literature review you will need to use some kind of method to organise your literature, otherwise it is very easy to feel as though you are lost and swimming around in so many sources. Half the battle with a literature review is being organised. Ways of organising your literature might be:

- Colour coding with highlighters or sticky notes.
- Storing particular papers in carefully labelled folders on a computer/cloud.
- Keeping some sources on a virtual 'shelf' or other kind of filing system or software that your university may have for you to use – for example, RefWorks (your library may be able to offer you training sessions to learn how to use such software).
- By using more 'old-fashioned' ways such as cue cards, whereby you summarise key details of each study on a small piece of paper, or a large-scale table such as the example in Table 9.2, which may help you to identify patterns based on the prevalence or scarcity of issues within the literature.

Structuring a literature review

You might think that organising and structuring a piece of work is of lesser importance than the actual content, but the reality is that the structure can make or break the work. If you can identify what the key overarching themes are and then decide what level of breadth and depth each theme is going to encompass, you can start to create a really coherent piece of work. To create your themes, group together similar issues that are at a smaller level and think about what kind of broader, overarching theme they could be classified under. Table 9.2 illustrates how the particular findings from specific studies can be categorised under broader themes.

Although you must clarify with your tutor or consult the assessment brief as to what the exact requirements or recommendations are, typically a literature review will comprise of:

- An **introduction**, to tell the reader what the scope and purpose of the work is. You may be asked to present research questions that have guided your enquiry into the literature.

Table 9.2 Organising literature themes and identifying patterns

Research paper	Methodology	Theme 1: Vulnerability	Theme 2: Pregnancy and STIs	Theme 3: Health-oriented approach predominant	Notes
Paper 1: Abbott et al. (2016) 'We've got a lack of family values': an examination of how teachers formulate and justify their approach to teaching sex and relationships education, *Sex Education* Vol. 16, No. 6, pp. 678–691	One-to-one interviews with teachers with a range of SRE training Sample: 8	Strong awareness of some pupils and characteristics of their lives that made them more vulnerable	Risks of teenage pregnancy and STIs were still a driving factor that influenced how teachers framed and delivered SRE	Health-related issues prioritised which potentially precludes other issues part of more comprehensive SRE	*Part of a wider study* *Authors suggest teachers need to reflect on their own possible assumptions*
Paper 2:					

- Some **rationale** for the work, or the area of focus.
- An **indicator of the structure** or sections the reader can expect, and possibly a comment or guidance upon what kinds of literature have been included in the review, or any particular approach taken.
- The **main body** (probably comprising around 80% of the work) which is **organised according to the key themes** you have identified: you will need to clarify whether it is expected, or acceptable for you to use subheadings in your work or not.
- A **conclusion** that should summarise your key findings really succinctly and offer some kind of judgement or appraisal on the overall state of the literature on your chosen topic. Here is also often a good place to flag up areas that you feel would benefit from further research.

Writing a literature review

Within each of the themes you have identified, your writing needs to do much more than just describe and present the key findings of that particular study. The trap to avoid is the 'shopping list' approach where each piece of literature is introduced and described in turn, in isolation, as this can only ever be a descriptive exercise which simply won't gain you many marks.

- Consider the issues you have to discuss within each theme and step back from writing about what each study has found in detail.
- A literature review is more concerned with trends, commonalities and differences found *across* a number of sources as opposed to within one particular source at a time.
- A key aim is to compare and contrast what different sources have to say about the same (or very similar) issues.
- Other characteristics you can incorporate into a literature review or questions to ask include:
  - If one piece of literature presents a particular viewpoint or claim, what do any other sources have to say about this same issue? We cannot make authoritative claims about a particular issue if we only have one source to support our claim with.
  - Can you comment upon the prominence of an issue across several different studies? That is, might we say 'many' studies or 'the majority' of studies identify or find a particular point?
  - Is a point or finding particularly interesting, relevant or topical, even though it is a minority point of view in the literature?
  - Is there a scarcity of research about a particular issue? Why might this be?
  - Are there certain researchers or theorists whose names and work feature prominently? Or, perhaps there are some studies or names that are cited frequently within the literature, and thus you know that you should seek out their work.
  - Is there anything to note about the particular trends in the literature with regard to publication dates (e.g. was there a flurry of activity in this area around a particular time period or very little before a certain date)?
  - Perhaps studies in a particular area tend to be largely derived from a particular country or part of the world? Is this significant?

o Have most studies taken a particular approach or used a particular methodology? Have some sections of society or participants with particular characteristics been excluded from existing research?

All of these points should help you to move away from being tempted to spend too long describing what various studies did and found – although it can be very valuable to include succinct examples from particular studies, or perhaps a quotation or point that illustrates a discussion or point of view effectively.

The language used in a literature review can sometimes be a little unfamiliar to students, as it can often be a challenge to think about how to present points in a varied manner, while retaining an academic style.

ACTIVITY 9.3

Language for a literature review

Think back to the example excerpts from Hek (2005) and Dearden and Becker (2002) earlier in this section, and the kinds of phrases used to introduce issues or ideas from the literature to the reader. Such phrasing may include:

- Many studies suggest that ...
- Literature in this area commonly recognises ...
- A minority of studies refer to ...
- More recent studies approach this issue from the perspective of ...
- There is evidence to suggest that several studies concur with this viewpoint ...
- In contrast, other studies surmise that ...

Can you think of any other suitable phrases that would be appropriate? It can be difficult to frequently present a new issue to the reader, but try to vary the language you use.

More substantial pieces of work: dissertations, final-year projects, extended writing

In addition to essay assignments, Education courses will often have longer and more substantial pieces of work of approximately 8,000–10,000 words, extending to 15,000–20,000 words at Master's level. Different courses have different requirements and terminology but usually these extended assignments are referred to as research projects, dissertations, final-year projects or extended writing pieces. It is common for students to undertake dissertations and research projects in the third year of undergraduate degrees and during Master's degrees. Often, a dissertation, final-year project or an extended piece of writing will contribute to a significant amount of assessment credits for the year as opposed to the value of just one module or unit of study.

Undertaking this substantial piece of work in your final year of study demonstrates students' ability to plan, design and undertake some data collection before analysing and presenting findings and recommendations on theoretical and/or practical levels.

Some courses may also have a research project assignment in years one and two, although these are usually shorter word lengths, for example 3,500–4,000 words. It is important for you to check what terminology is used on your course/university and the word limit requirements.

Dissertations or final-year projects and extended pieces of writing are different to essays. As they are longer pieces of work they tend to have more structure to help guide and focus the reader. To give more structure and guide the reader they contain chapters, headings and subheadings as well as the signposting strategy that we have discussed in Chapter 6.

A dissertation

Undertaking a dissertation research project enables you to focus on an in-depth study of a particular area of Educational Research that you have developed during your studies at university. Working with a supervisor or tutor (like the terminology of projects, the name of the person supervising you can vary from institution to institution) you will often have the opportunity to build on a personal interest that you have been developing throughout the course. This might be a particular topic that you've developed a special interest in during your first- and/or second-year modules, a research method you encountered when looking at research methods or a sense of curiosity sparked by an experience on a placement or while volunteering. Some students also conduct small-scale studies into areas where there are links to their aspirations following graduation – for example, undertaking research on behaviour management strategies, evaluating and developing inclusive practices in the classroom or exploring media representations of women in sport and the impact of this upon female pupils' aspirations. Students have found that undertaking such an approach and linking it to what they see themselves doing in the future enables them to discuss their ideas and research at job, further study and Initial Teacher Education (ITE) interviews.

Narrowing down the topic

Once you have decided on an area of interest that you wish to explore and know the structure required, another important decision to make is whether you would like to conduct an empirical study where you would use research methods to generate and collect primary data (e.g. collecting participants' perspectives about particular educational issues) before analysing it or complete a conceptual desk-based study where you draw on and analyse secondary data (e.g. literature, datasets and policy documents). Although both types of project require you to undertake some research and analyse data, the research design, methodology and analytical framework you use will be very different. Your supervisor will be able to give you advice and guidance about which type of project is most appropriate for you, your interests and your studies.

After you have identified the topic area that you would like to explore, it is likely that you will need to narrow down the focus of your research to make sure the project is manageable and at an appropriate level for the stage you're at with your studies. You need to create a research question or some questions to operationalise your research project (Cohen et al., 2017). There are different kinds of questions we can ask and they will determine the participants, the design of the study and the analysis process. Thomas (2009, p. 6) highlights that questions can help to understand 'what is the situation?', 'what is going on?', 'what happens when?' and 'what is related to what?'.

You may initially feel overwhelmed by all of the research studies and existing literature published about your area of research; do not panic as this is a perfectly normal feeling. What you need to do is create a system so that you can effectively identify a focus of your research within the topic area. Some questions to ask yourself are:

- What topic am I interested in?
- What interests me specifically about this topic?
- Identify specific key words and concepts in a title.
- What are you interested in in terms of the purpose of the research – for example, is it to explore, to identify, to consider the relationship between two or more concepts?

When thinking about these questions try to remember what topics you have enjoyed studying on your course and why. Is there a particular topic that you've enjoyed reading about and developed since your first year? Have you recently discovered a new interest that you feel passionate about since undertaking a placement or voluntary work? This process will help you to identify specific research questions. As we have discussed earlier in this chapter, undertaking a literature review will help you to identify any gaps in the research field and formulate your guiding research questions.

What makes a good research question (or set of questions)?

Thomas (2017) identifies that research questions are at the heart of any research and they will help your project to take shape and guide you through the process to completion. To create some questions you need to know what it is that you want your research to address or what you want to find out. You then need to think about the best way to ask the question. Generally, good research questions (or a set of questions) will include the following:

- One or two main questions with no more than two or three sub-questions that will help to address the main one(s).
- 'What' and 'why' type questions.
- Using words to highlight the nature of the research – for example, 'discover', 'explore'.

It is important to check that your research questions can be answered and that the answers stem from the data (Cohen et al., 2017). You should make sure the questions are not too big or too narrow and that they link to the data collected.

In addition to demonstrating your knowledge, understanding and ability to undertake a research project, the assessment of the dissertation may also include:

- Whether the work shows evidence of the writer identifying a relevant area to research and appropriate research questions.
- The level of critical engagement with a range of literature.
- A sensitivity to the process of data collection and associated ethical issues.
- The relevance of the data collection and data analysis to the research questions.
- Whether the writer has developed an argument beyond description and unsubstantiated opinion.
- If there is an appropriate structure and coherence relevant to the dissertation and usual research conventions.
- The standard of presentation of the work and the accuracy of references.

(This guidance was taken from the Year 3 BA Education Dissertation module handbook at the University of East Anglia and different courses may vary so please check with your lecturer.)

After reading the list above you may be wondering what the 'usual research conventions' are. Research conventions can vary depending on the type of research carried out, although generally dissertations or project reports should include the chapters or sections respectively given in Table 9.3.

Table 9.3	Typical breakdown of dissertation chapters for a study involving primary data collection
Chapters (these may also be called sections)	**What to include**
Abstract	A clear and concise summary of the research project. This short section of approximately 150–200 words should highlight the headlines of your research, e.g. a brief background to provide a context for the reader, the methodology and analysis, findings and brief conclusions.
Table of contents	Information about page numbers for chapters and sections. Page numbers for figures, tables and charts should be listed separately.
Acknowledgements	This isn't always a requirement; it's more of a kind piece of writing to thank those people who have supported you throughout the research process and writing of the project, e.g. family and friends, the participants (but remember to keep them anonymous or use pseudonyms), your supervisor and even your pets (if you wish to)!
Introduction	The research aims and objectives and research questions. You should also provide a background to the research project, e.g. relevant literature or a personal rationale, e.g. why you were interested in carrying out the piece of research (remember to keep it critical rather than descriptive).
Literature review	A systematic review of a range of literature relevant to the research field that the topic is located in. It should identify gaps in the existing literature.

Chapters (these may also be called sections)	What to include
Methodology and data analysis (sometimes these are presented as individual chapters)	Outlines the methodological approach and methods used to generate and collect the data and should include the following: • The methodological approach and research design, e.g. qualitative or quantitative and the methods used (e.g. interviews, focus groups, questionnaires, observations). There should also be a substantiated discussion about why particular methods were chosen and others were discounted (this will help you to demonstrate knowledge and understanding of how to conduct a study). • Information about the sample, sample size and context, e.g. the type of setting and area it is located within. Usually it is vital to ensure the anonymity of the participants here and settings shouldn't be identifiable. • Information about the research process, e.g. how the research was carried out. The information given should enable the study to be replicated by someone else. There should also be a discussion about the reliability and validity of the study as well as any generalisability claims and your reflexivity as a researcher. • A consideration of any ethical issues and/or concerns. Here, state the ethical guidelines and processes which underpin the project and address these (universities usually require students to complete and ethics application to gain ethical clearance).
	The data analysis section (or separate chapter) includes information about how the data will be analysed, e.g. thematic analysis and the procedure undertaken (such as what themes were identified). This section/chapter will look different, especially depending on whether you are conducting an empirical or conceptual desk-based study (please see section below).
Findings Results (if a quantitative study)	Presents your findings or results, what you have found out from undertaking the research. These may be presented as quotations from participants and images if the research is qualitative or charts and graphs if a quantitative approach has been taken. You can also combine the two if the research is mixed-methods.
Discussion	Here you discuss the findings/results in relation to the research questions and wider research field. It is an opportunity to contextualise your findings with previous research.
Conclusion	This summarises the research and dissertation. There should also be sections on the limitations of the research and recommendations (e.g. for practice and/or future research).
References	This is the list of references that you have cited in the dissertation/report.
Appendices	At the end of your dissertation/project this is the space where you can include materials that you have used, e.g. anonymised ethics application, questionnaire and interview instruments, images collected as part of the findings and an interview/focus group transcript.

A research report and an extended essay/piece of writing

These types of writing have a similar structure to a dissertation as you will be presenting a research study, illustrating the findings and discussing these in relation to the wider educational research field. However, the contents – for example, 'Introduction', 'Literature Review', 'Methodology' and so on – will be sections rather than chapters. A research report may also be a shorter piece of writing – for example, 4000–5000 words (but this will vary from course to course).

Planning, organising and researching such a large piece of work: setting a schedule and time frames

As with any writing task, planning is key! Although the task of writing 8,000–10,000 words (and probably more for a Master's dissertation) may be overwhelming at first, many students say that they wish they had more words to 'play with' towards the end of the drafting and writing process.

> **TIP**
>
> **A word about word count**
>
> Courses will also vary in terms of what is included and excluded in the word count. You should find out from your supervisor/tutor whether components such as the titles, abstract, references (reference list) and appendices are counted on your course.

Breaking down the task and setting time frames are really important. University courses will vary in terms of the time period for undertaking a research task and writing up the findings, but usually the project completion time spans over at least a semester or term if not an academic year (e.g. September to May/June). Similarly to the time management involved with planning and writing an essay that we identified and discussed in Chapter 6, the dissertation report or extended essay time management can follow a similar structure. Table 9.4 is an example of what a time frame for an academic year might look like (however, you should always plan a time frame schedule with your research project or dissertation supervisor).

From week 8 the time frame is an approximation because the timing of the activities depends on the data collection process. Some students collect all of their data in two weeks and others require two months. You should discuss your time frame with your tutor or supervisor. The reality is that you may also have other deadlines during the writing-up process as well so it is important to keep to a schedule and complete work on the research project when you are able to. If you do find that you have some free time earlier in the schedule, make sure you use it to complete tasks rather than leaving everything until the deadline.

Table 9.4	A typical dissertation or project planning timeline		
Time frame	**Activity**	**Draft activities**	**Words (Approx.)**
Weeks 1–5	Think about a research topic Review existing research literature and policy documents. It is also important to think about methodology and ethical considerations during this period (you should still consider ethical issues if you are undertaking a desk-based study).	Literature review and research questions.	2,000–2,500
Weeks 5–6	Ethics application.	Ethics documents (courses will vary in terms of what this includes – ask your research project supervisor).	Check your university requirement.
Weeks 6–8	Focus on methodology and refining research instruments (e.g. interview and focus group schedules or questionnaire items). Also contact any participants to begin arranging when data generation and collection can take place.	Methodology chapter/ section (include here a discussion of any ethical considerations and the data analysis process). Develop instruments to generate and collect data.	2,000
Week 8 onwards Week 14–15 onwards (although this will vary depending on your data collection – you need to allow time for this and possibly to rearrange times if participants need to rearrange or maybe even withdraw from the study).	Data generation and collection Data analysis – this can be a continual process which takes place during the data collection if you have enough data.	Write up data analysis process and include any codes and themes identified.	
Weeks 16–20	Focus on research findings and locating these within the existing research field.	Findings/results and discussion chapters/ sections. Presentation of data in themes	3,500

Timeframe	Activity	Draft activities	Words (Approx.)
		Interpretation, analysis and discussion of your data. This discussion will link your findings to literature on the topic. Reviewing literature review chapter.	
Week 21	Think about the conclusion. Summary of key findings and what their significance is. Limitations of the study and things you'd do differently if you were to do the research again. Directions and suggestions for practice (if applicable) and further research.	Write the concluding chapter/section.	1,000
Week 22	Think about an introductory chapter. What is the research topic and why are you interested in it? What are the research questions and why are these significant?	Write the introduction chapter/section.	1,000
Week 23	Organising references and appendices.		These are not included in the word count usually. However, always check with your supervisor.
Week 24	Final check – consistency of the research message and spelling, punctuation and grammar.		

As you may be juggling different pieces of work and deadlines it is also a good idea to make a note of the points discussed with your supervisor during the tutorials. Although you will be meeting regularly with your project tutor/supervisor, it's a good idea to keep a record of important feedback and actions to help you with your research process.

Preparing for tutorials

Tutorials will vary between courses in terms of length of time and what is discussed during them. The main objective of a tutorial is to help the student to develop their knowledge and understanding of their research project. This may be in terms of reviewing the literature, thinking carefully about the methodology, looking at and ways to analyse any data and then thinking about what this means in the wider Educational Research field. You could be asked to submit a draft piece of work to your supervisor to read before your tutorial and this will be discussed during the tutorial (although this will vary between different courses). At the beginning of the research process, your tutor may ask more of the questions to guide the discussion but by the middle to the end of the process you should be guiding the discussion.

Preparation is key! Questions to ask during a tutorial

Thinking about questions to ask before tutorials will help you to maximise the benefits of the time spent with your project tutor/supervisor. It's useful to think about questions in relation to specific tasks or chapter writing and try to avoid asking 'yes/no' and closed types of questions. Here are some potential questions you could ask your supervisor to get you started:

- I've done lots of reading, how can I structure this into a literature review?
- Have I referred to literature appropriately in my literature review?
- How should I phrase my research question(s)?
- I think this is the most appropriate method to use to collect the data because … Do you agree?
- Is my argument clearly presented? How can I make my argument more prominent?
- How can I analyse my data?
- Is my consideration of ethical precautions sufficient?

Your questions will change and develop throughout the research process. It's useful to keep a reflective diary alongside undertaking your research so that you can make a note of any questions to ask your project tutor/supervisor.

You will notice that the writing activities are all in draft form (except the ethics application). This is because when writing a dissertation, research project or an extended essay you should try to keep an open mind and keep revising the work until there is a consistent message that is clearly presented throughout all of the chapters. It might be that after you have analysed your data you need to revise your literature review and so on.

Towards the end of the research and drafting process (when you have your findings or results) you will begin to see the 'bigger picture' of your research – you will have an overview of what you wanted to do, why you did it (from a research perspective), how you did it, what the findings are and what this means for practice and/or future directions for research. As with other writing tasks, use signposting to connect the end of one chapter with the beginning of another. You should also link chapters within the writing – for example, 'as stated in Chapter 2 ... .' or 'in the following chapter ...'.

At this point you need to take a closer look at the content of your draft chapters or sections and check that they are all giving a consistent message. Some key questions to ask include:

- Are the research questions clearly stated at the beginning and end of the piece of writing?
- Are the research questions answered?
- Does the argument run throughout all of the chapters, and is the argument clear?
- Is there an introduction and summary at the beginning and end of each chapter?

Once you have edited and revised (possibly following a number of edits) the dissertation, research project or extended piece of writing, you should reflect and evaluate upon it before submitting it. Here is a checklist for you to consider:

✓ Does the work show evidence of the writer identifying a relevant area to research?
✓ Are the research questions clearly stated at various points in the writing?
✓ Is the literature critically reviewed rather than just described?
✓ Is there a rationale for the methodology and methods used?
✓ Is the data collection and analysis process clear?
✓ Is the data relevant to the research questions?
✓ Are the arguments supported by relevant literature and evidence?
✓ Is there an appropriate structure?
✓ Are all of the references included?

Chapter summary: useful points for you to implement

- Although every kind of assignment covered in this chapter has different characteristics and requirements, be reassured that you're not starting from scratch each time, as all written work in an Education programme has many kinds of similarities, such as demonstrating skills of analysis, criticality and evidence of your research. By refining these skills, you will become adept at altering your style, tone and approach to an assignment, depending on its type.
- Taking the time to structure and plan your work carefully is effort well-spent, and will make the process of assessment much less stressful.

Receiving and Using Feedback Effectively

You will have received various forms of feedback in your previous education and possibly employment and you will need to be able to respond to it in the future when you are working in your chosen career. This feedback may take many different forms and you need to develop your skills so that you are ready to be able to deal with it, respond to it and act on it. The feedback you receive at university is central to your learning and development. In this chapter we will focus on:

- Why feedback is important.
- Forms of feedback.
- How to respond to feedback.
- Demystifying assessment feedback and criteria.
- How to use feedback effectively throughout your course.

Why is feedback important?

In the feedback you receive from your lecturers and other sources such as your peers, you will gain information about your knowledge and understanding while studying Education. Through feedback you will learn to understand the strengths of your work and what you need to work on to develop your abilities further. As researchers have highlighted, it can be a way in which you can develop an understanding of the assessment criteria (Norton et al., 2009), the rules of academic writing and crucially what the different ways of writing 'academically' mean (Northedge, 2003). However, research has also highlighted that feedback can be confusing because of mismatches between student and lecturer understandings of the requirements of essay writing and the assessment of this (Lea and Street, 1998; Williams, 2005). Therefore, it is really important that students and lecturers share an understanding of the feedback, in addition to the assignment task briefs. In this chapter, you'll learn about the different types of feedback that you might receive and how you can use feedback effectively. As well as exploring the different types of feedback, we'll look at student reactions to it, share tips and strategies for dealing with comments (particularly written feedback) and suggest ways in which you can have an input into the feedback process and have your questions answered to gain a better understanding of the feedback you receive.

A student's perspective: How to reflect on comments from lecturers

Formative feedback is so helpful prior to writing summative assignments. In particular, it highlights what you are doing really well and therefore what you should continue to do, but also identifies areas for improvement. This is so useful as it is an opportunity to improve your writing/presentation skills before you are marked on them, enabling you to get the best mark you possibly can. I always use my formative feedback when writing my assignments so that I am constantly improving upon previous errors and to ensure I do not make the same mistakes again. It is also great practice for the real thing and allows you to develop necessary skills before you are actually marked!

(Third-year Education Student)

There are two main modes of feedback that students often receive on their work: during the assignment and after you have handed it in. Comments about your work while you are developing your ideas can help you to develop assignments before you submit them for a final assessment. You may not receive a mark for this work (a formative piece of work). Some students are unmotivated to complete work before the final assessment if they do not get a mark for it. However, as the student's experience illustrates, the formative feedback is important to the overall learning process.

The feedback you receive after you have submitted your work for final marking will usually include comments from your lecturer and an overall mark. This mark is used to assess your performance and the feedback comments should illustrate to what extent and how well you've met the learning outcomes and the specified assessment criteria – for example, the level of knowledge and understanding and criticality within the piece of work. It can also identify any next steps that you can take in future pieces of work to try and improve in future assessments. You can also view feedback that you receive about summative work in a formative way. This is because although the lecturer comments are about one piece of work, often the advice can be relevant and applicable to assignments you will complete in the future, even in different modules. For example, the lecturer's comments may have given guidance about being critical in your writing and using research literature as evidence to support the points being made in the argument in an assignment. Although it is always important to discuss work with your lecturers, such guidance can be applied to a range of assessments.

Forms of feedback

There are various forms that feedback can take. Written comments on your assignments is not the only kind of feedback you will receive from your lecturers. However, let's start with written feedback because this might be the most obvious way that you think you'll receive feedback about your work and the progress you're

A student's perspective: Using summative feedback in an (in)formative way

It took me a while to realise that feedback I received for summative work, usually at the end of a module, could help me with writing for other modules. I'm so glad I do though. Just because it's feedback at the end of a module, it doesn't mean it isn't useful for other assignments. Lecturers will often write about the structure of my work and what I can do to make it better, and how I can introduce sources better to support my arguments. I can use this information to help me with other assignments. Otherwise it's a wasted opportunity!

(Second-year Education Student)

making in your developing knowledge and understanding about education. Yet, as we will explore, there are other forms of feedback that can be equally, and sometimes (depending on the context) more, effective.

Written comments

Usually once you've submitted your work for final assessment written comments will accompany a mark at the end of a piece of writing or on an assessment feedback form. This can be presented in a variety of ways, from a handwritten coversheet to a highlighted rubric with online marking. You should ask your lecturers and tutors how you can expect to receive your feedback. Generally, the comments will:

- Identify the strengths and weaknesses of the piece of work.
- Give guidance and next steps about how you can improve your work in future (e.g. Could you have been more critical and drawn on a wider range of academic readings to give alternative viewpoints?).
- Provide a justification for the mark given (if it is a summative assessment).

Sometimes lecturers will also provide written annotations on your work. They will often refer to these in the overall written feedback comments and they can help learners to contextualise the meaning of what their lecturers are highlighting. Sometimes you may not fully understand what your feedback is telling you. For example, it may say that you need to be 'more critical to achieve a higher grade' but you may not understand what it means to be more critical. If there is something that you don't understand, you should ask your tutors to explain it further. If you have any questions about the written comments you should speak to the lecturer who marked your work to avoid any misunderstandings.

Discussing assignments with your tutors

Tutorials are another useful way for gaining feedback and also clarifying feedback from your lecturers. Lecturers may seem very authoritative and the prospect of talking to them can seem daunting to some students. However, they are still people, they are approachable and will really appreciate the opportunity to talk about Education and to help you to improve your knowledge and understanding of topics and assessment practices. In fact, talking to them about your feedback is another excellent resource. It will enable you to develop your knowledge and understanding further and you can ask questions to help you to improve future assignments.

The focus of tutorials and the way they are structured varies from lecturer to lecturer and also across courses and institutions. Usually lecturers hold office hours, a weekly set period of time where students can meet with them to discuss any questions about course content or assessments. At other times a lecturer may ask students to prepare some notes or submit an annotated plan before the tutorial to be discussed in the tutorial. When you go to a tutorial it is important that you are prepared (e.g. you have done some thinking and planning beforehand) and have a list of the questions you would like to ask and the things that you would like to discuss. You should also be prepared to talk about your thoughts and ideas because tutorials are a fantastic opportunity for you to think aloud, articulate your thoughts and ask your lecturers for advice about how to improve. As Neil Mercer (2000, p. 98) suggested, 'reasoning is visible in the talk'. Before going to a tutorial you might wish to consider the following tips:

- Plan the tutorial. What topics would you like to discuss? What do you already know and what would you like further guidance on?
- If you have an assignment coming up you could take a plan with you and ask specific questions about the structure and whether there is evidence of critical analysis.
- Do not just ask questions such as 'Have I done this right?', as these kinds of questions tend to yield 'yes' and/or 'no' responses and these will not be useful for developing your understanding.
- Try and be specific about what you would like help and guidance with. Lecturers and tutors can only give you guidance if they know what you're struggling with.

A student's perspective: Making the most of tutorials

How do I prepare for tutorials? In terms of preparing for a tutorial, I always ensure I have brought with me any relevant notes/books. This is because I find a great deal can be discussed in tutorials, and I want to ensure I can discuss fully anything that may arise. If I have been struggling or want to discuss something in particular, I try to write this down so I don't forget to mention it. I also find it beneficial to spend 5/10 minutes alone before a tutorial thinking about what I want to discuss. This ensures I'm in the right mind going into the session. I always go in with the intention of writing notes during the tutorial, however these sessions turn into much more of a discussion where I get more from talking alone. Speaking out loud with another person is really valuable in itself, especially when it's with a tutor who can guide you in the right direction. Saying that, I do think it's essential to write notes immediately after so the key themes discussed aren't forgotten. If possible, I like to go to the library immediately after while I have the tutorial discussion on my mind.

(Third-year Education Student)

You could also begin a dialogue with your lecturers before you submit work to receive feedback. As mentioned earlier, lecturers will be happy to talk about their subject discipline(s) with students and the assessment process. A student once asked me 'How do you know what I'd like feedback on, you haven't asked me?' and I thought this is very true and I embed opportunities for students to ask questions within their courses. This may be during lectures, seminars and tutorials and also prior to the submission of formative and summative coursework. Try and find out what opportunities there are within your courses.

Conversations, debates and discussions in lectures and seminars and outside teaching sessions

You can also ask your lecturers questions in lectures and seminars. Some students may not feel confident doing this though and may prefer to use tutorials. In sessions you may also receive feedback from your peers (as well as your lecturers and tutors in seminars). Seminars are an opportunity for you to try out your learning of new concepts and ideas and to develop and consolidate your knowledge and understanding by rehearsing educational perspectives and arguments. Feedback from lecturers and peers may also be given via online discussion boards. You can also email questions to your lecturers (and this may sometimes be a quicker way of getting a response than waiting for their office hours or your next teaching session).

Peer feedback (formal and informal)

As course friends, peers can also give and receive invaluable feedback to each other by acting as 'critical friends'. As critical friends you can help each other to think about the key educational ideas and concepts in a deeper way and ask questions to extend thinking. Similarly to tutorials, discussing ideas among friends can help to identify any gaps in understanding as well as extending thinking. Some helpful questions might be:

- Can you talk through the topic?
- Can you give some examples?
- What does the research literature say about the topic? Are there any gaps or contradictions?
- Is there anything you do not understand?

It's important that the questioning doesn't lead to just 'yes' or 'no' responses because these types of questions could hinder the thought processes and shut down any learning rather than help to expand it.

How to respond to feedback

As we mentioned earlier in this book, studying an Education subject at university may be a completely new subject for you. Although you may have studied subjects within disciplines such as Psychology, Sociology, History, Philosophy and Politics before, Education is an interdisciplinary subject and requires students to think critically about many aspects from each of those subjects.

Adjusting to this may have an impact on your writing and marks as well as the way you think about studying. Do check your Course Handbook to find out what your grade or percentage means, as this can differ from university to university. However, it is not helpful to fixate on the mark as this number or letter grade only shows you what you attained on one piece of work, at one point in time; it doesn't tell you how to improve – it is the lecturers' comments, their feedback on your work which will help you with this. Often students decide not to read the comments on a piece of work if they are unhappy or dissatisfied with the grade. It is understandable that people will be disappointed with a low mark, particularly if they feel they have put a lot of effort into a piece of work and this does not then seem to be reflected in the mark. You may also think that the comments are harsh and critical of you as a person because you have written the work. However, rather than being discouraged, you should read the lecturer's comments and any annotations written within the text because they will offer guidance and tell you how you could possibly improve your academic work.

TIP

Dealing with feedback

If you are feeling upset, disappointed, frustrated or angry with your lecturer's comments about a piece of work, don't just file it away or even worse put it in the bin (even though this might be what you would like to do with it)! Instead, leave it for a little while (a couple of hours or a day) and then go back to it with a more objective frame of mind. Remember that the feedback is commenting on your work and not you personally so try to not be defensive when reading the comments. Try and look at the feedback in a more positive way – it is there to help you so think about how each comment can help you to improve your work. It is useful to write out the comments in your own hand writing and in your own words so that the feedback then becomes your own. You are then ready to begin to understand it.

At the other end of the scale, learners should also look at their lecturer's comments about their work even if they are pleased with the mark. Similarly to students who are disappointed with their marks, there is also a tendency among students who have received a good mark to not read the feedback. While it is nice to enjoy the satisfactory glow of doing well and achieving a good grade, it is still important to read the feedback because the lecturer comments may provide guidance on further ways in which the work can be improved in future assignments, and possibly assessments within different modules. If you are receiving grades within the 60s and 70s strive for more and learn how to possibly improve your academic writing further and get marks in the 80s and possibly 90s!

TIP

How to act on feedback. Consider:

- Do you always read your lecturer feedback?
- What impacts on the way you read it, and how you act on it?
- How could you make better use of your lecturer's comments?

Regardless of the marks you have achieved it is important to reflect on the lecturer comments and create an action plan. This will help learners to make sense of the feedback and to think about what they need to improve on in preparation for future assignments, whether they are within the same module or a different module. You might wish to use the template given in Figure 10.1 to help organise your reflections.

What have I learnt from the lecturer feedback?

Things to think about...

Questions to ask my lecturer to help me improve...

Next steps to help me improve...

Figure 10.1   Sample feedback template

Making sense of feedback – Reflecting on the comments

1   Have the assignment task brief/question and assessment criteria to hand.
2   Read through your work and the comments.
3   If the work is a summative assessment, look at the assessment criteria and carefully consider if you understand why your lecturer has given your work the mark they have.
4   Read through each comment and check that you understand what your lecturer has written and the reason why they have written it. At this point it might also be useful to check any annotations on your work as these may give you additional examples of how you can improve your writing.
5   Cottrell (2008, p. 218) advises learners to create two columns:
   (a) Major issues – areas which lose A LOT of marks, e.g. not answering the question; lack of evidence; poor argument; weak structure.
   (b) Minor errors – areas where you will not lose lots of marks but they are important to the overall presentation of your assignment and can help you achieve more marks.
6   Go through your tutor comments listing them as either 'major' or 'minor' issues and number them in order of priority areas to work on.
7   Think about how you can improve the priority areas you have identified.
8   **If you're unsure of anything, ask your lecturer for advice and guidance (helping you to understand is one of their many roles). You can also approach your university study skills/learning enhancement centre to talk about your feedback if you're not sure what your tutor's comments mean.**

It is a good idea for you to keep a record of any phrases or words used within the feedback that you do not understand or those which keep reoccurring. For example, we have started our own one in Table 10.1. This active engagement with the feedback vocabulary will help learners to understand what they are being asked to do and how to improve. Again, if there are any words or phrases that are not clear or familiar, learners should ask their lecturers.

Demystifying assessment and feedback phrases

Once learners have a greater understanding of the assessment criteria and what the lecturer comments in the feedback mean it is then possible to make an action plan to improve knowledge and understanding of key educational ideas and issues and how to demonstrate this using academic writing. With this knowledge and understanding, you can then use the feedback to 'feed-forward' into future essays and assignments.

Table 10.1 Examples of feedback phrases	
Word/Phrase	**What it means**
'More critical analysis needed'	Drawing on literature or other academic sources to clearly present an argument. Looking at the arguments/findings and writing about what they mean. Asking the 'so what?' question (refer back to Chapter 6)
'Where is your academic tone?'	Tone is a writer's voice. For it to be an 'academic tone' the voice should be formal and objective, e.g. no slang words (refer back to Chapter 7)
'Synthesis'	Putting parts together to make a new whole, e.g. 'synthesising literature' would require a review of different studies and bringing this information together to create/develop an argument
'Learning outcomes'	What you are required to do to demonstrate learning in an assignment

'FeedForward'

Interpreting and understanding feedback to 'feedforward'

Summary of lecturers' comments

Module 1: Formative assignment 1 and 2: More detail required on research methods. I need to provide more clarity with regard to what I mean. *Summative 1:* More detail/illustrations required. Discussion needs to be focused. *Summative 2:* Argument tends to be one-sided. The assignment would have benefited if I had been more critical. Standard of English is good but I need to consider my choice of words. I need to be mindful of repeating myself.

Module 2: Essay would have benefited from covering less and providing more detail in what was covered.

Module 3: Overall I needed more depth and to expand on the points made.

Module 4: Points need expanding. Ensure everything is supported with evidence.

Student's action plan

This semester I am going to focus on covering fewer points in essays but provide more information on the points I do make. I will also get a friend/family member to read my assignments to ensure clarity. I will ensure that all of my work is critical.

When the feedback makes more sense it is easier to act upon it and put it into practice in future essays and other assignments. This can be for either assessments where you can get comments from your tutors during the drafting and writing process or when you have submitted a piece for final assessment and you're thinking about the next assignment(s). Assessments where you can get comments from your tutors and lecturers during the process are ideal pieces to try out new ideas and ways of writing as you may receive further feedback on drafts or annotated plans before completing and submitting work for summative assessment. Formative assessment doesn't count towards your overall grade and you will receive guidance to enable you to develop your skills even further.

Using feedback effectively for the rest of your course

In this chapter we have looked at the different types of feedback, how learners can deal with and understand feedback and how they can put their lecturer's comments into practice to improve their learning and academic writing for use in future assignments. A key message throughout this chapter is that for feedback to be effective, you need to use it! Refer to it and use it across assignments, modules and possibly courses if you are studying a joint honours degree. Although some modules may be different with different learning outcomes it is important to not overlook the feedback. There may be some information about stylistic features and referencing and these may be applicable across modules (but if in doubt, check with your lecturer). There are also some tips and strategies to ensure feedback is a feature of the lifelong learning process. As we mentioned at the beginning of the chapter, you will need to receive and respond to feedback once you have completed your degree in your future career.

Using a reflective journal to help manage feedback

In a similar way to reflecting on lecturers' written comments about assignments, it is useful to reflect on all of the feedback learners receive from their lecturers and also their peers. One way to do this is to use a reflective journal. The important thing about a reflective journal is that it enables learners to critically reflect on what is important to them. So, it should be personal to individual learners although the example questions in the tip box below might be a useful starting point when thinking about reflecting on feedback from various sources (e.g. written comments, tutorials and peer-to-peer activities).

TIP

Examples of questions for the reflective journal

- What is the feedback like?
- What do I think and feel about the feedback?
- What went well with the assignment? What went less well?
- What have I learnt from the feedback?
- Are there any patterns or themes emerging across assignments and/or modules?
- Targets to focus on and how are you going to develop?

Try to help yourself by devising really specific and tangible actions that will help you improve future work. So, rather than writing 'research more' for your next assignment, break this down into *how* you will go about undertaking more research. For example, beginning your research sooner; extending your reach further to include a greater number of sources; trying to obtain more statistical data to draw upon; reading from your sources in greater depth rather than just at a surface level (see Chapters 1 and 2).

In addition to reflecting on feedback from different sources, it is also useful to keep a note of the key messages from each assignment, both formative and summative ones.

A student's perspective: Keeping a journal and regular critical reflection

Before I start each assignment I refer back to feedback from the previous assignments and remain mindful of the comments whilst writing. I found this really helpful because it brought into focus what I need to do to improve my writing. As I've made notes on feedback from every assignment I can see where I am making similar errors, as well as what I'm doing well at. It's fresh in my mind what I need to focus on to improve and I can try and do that.

(Third-year Education Student)

As learners build up collections of reflections and catalogues of the key messages from feedback about academic writing and knowledge and understanding of Education as a discipline they should regularly share these. It is important as a self-regulated learner that students inform lecturers about the kind of feedback that they would find useful for their development in addition to the more generic feedback. Such a dialogue is important as it helps students to be engaged and motivated in the feedback and it gives lecturers and tutors an idea of what feedback is useful for students.

Chapter summary: useful points for you to implement

- Keep a copy of all feedback you receive so that you can return to it from time to time to observe how you have progressed or areas that you still need to work on.
- Do reflect on the feedback you receive for both formative and summative work. Remember feedback on summative work can help you to learn and develop your ideas and writing for your next assignment.
- While it can be useful to discuss feedback points with fellow students, do not get caught up in making too many comparisons between your work and someone else's. The person marking your work will have taken many things into account before assigning a grade and writing feedback, even though you think you should

have a higher grade than your friend because you have a longer reference list, it's never that straightforward.

- Don't forget that you can ask your tutors and lecturers questions about your work during the drafting and writing (or developing if it's a presentation, for example) process. You should expect to receive feedback when you are asked to complete assignments during this process as well as at the end once you have submitted your work for final grading.

Observing and Reflecting as an Education Student

Many Education programmes require students to reflect upon their own educational experiences and then analyse these from personal and theoretical perspectives. Being able to reflect and critically analyse your observations is a valuable key skill that can be immensely important on your course as well as in creating future reflective practitioners. As part of your course, you may well have the opportunity to observe in educational settings or scenarios and be required to critically reflect and analyse these at a number of different levels. We can all reflect, and we do so on a regular basis in our everyday lives, for example when we decide what our favourite meals are and why we like them or what the benefits of social media are. Reflecting upon and using personal experiences in your writing can help you to illustrate cases in your writing and demonstrate an understanding of the links between theory and practice.

Reflective Writing: Reflecting on Your Own Learning Experiences

Jennifer Moon (2010, p. 82) describes reflection as 'common-sense reflecting':

> a form of mental processing – like a form of thinking – that we may use to fulfil a purpose or to achieve some anticipated outcome or we may simply 'be reflective' and then an outcome can be unexpected.

Like essay writing, reflection is a process that supports our learning process. Key reflection theorists such as Dewey (1933), Kolb (1984) and Schon (1983) proposed that we learn through combinations of thought and action, reflection and practice, theory and application. In this chapter, we will look at:

- What reflection is.
- Why we reflect.
- Ways of reflecting.
- Linking your reflections to academic literature.
- Including and drawing on your reflections in your academic writing.

Reflection and the value of you reflecting on your experiences of education

Although you may not realise at the moment, you will have a wealth of experience to reflect on, both personally from being a learner and educated within formal and informal settings and maybe also from any opportunities you have had to develop work-based experiences in settings – for example, on a placement as part of your course or undertaking a volunteering role. The next chapter (Chapter 12) will specifically look at reflecting on observed experiences in practice/on placement.

Why do we reflect?

Take a moment to think about the reasons *why* we need to reflect on our experiences, or an issue, and see if you can note down three specific reasons in Activity 11.1.

Reasons to reflect as part of a degree programme

1 _____

2 _____

3 _____

See some suggested answers at the end of this chapter.

A student's perspective: How reflection and reflective thinking helped with academic writing

I believe that the characteristics of academic writing are precision, presentation and reflection. I wasn't aware of how vital reflection was until studying at university. It's a prominent part of most work, yet is not really something others may deem necessary. However, reflection in academic writing helps you to improve the way you view and reflect within practice.

Linked to this student's experience of the value of reflection, and reflecting upon her experiences in practice, reflection is important because it allows learners to engage with 'Higher Order Thinking' skills (see Bloom et al., 1956) such as 'analysis', 'synthesis' and 'evaluation'. Reflection enables students to develop these critical thinking skills which are invaluable for academic studies and employability. Within educational settings students can reflect on a situation and make demonstrable links between educational theories and what happens in practice.

What's the value of your own experiences?

Reflecting on a learning experience

Think about a learning experience and identify the different factors that were present within the experience. It can be a formal experience – for example, in a classroom or school setting – or an informal one – for example, learning to drive a car. You may find the following questions helpful:

- What?
- Why?
- What was your reaction?
- Were there any issues?
- Did you find anything challenging?
- What have you learned?

Your own experiences are very important to your own learning development journey. They will shape your perspectives and actions about many, if not all, the educational issues that you will encounter throughout the course of your degree. We have all participated in an education system whether it is in the UK or an international system, and the experiences we have accumulated will have an impact on the ways we think about education. Your experiences may be the reason why you're now studying an Education degree programme. You may have been inspired by a teacher in Primary School, or disaffected by your Secondary School Mathematics teacher, or interested by learning in an informal setting – for example, a Performing Arts group. Either way you may now be interested to try and make a difference to children and young people's educational lives, and to learn about the role of education within wider society to promote social justice. You do, however, need to make sure that any experiences you share within your assignments have an academic tone similar to the rest of your assignment. When reflections are included in writing there is a tendency to recall and be descriptive rather than critical and analytical. It is easy to slip into the 'I think' and 'I feel' mode of writing, and although the reflections are about your thoughts and feelings, they are a lot more than this being reflections, so the level of detail is important.

Levels of reflective writing

In a generic framework for Reflective Writing, Jennifer Moon (2010, pp. 214–216) highlights that there are four stages of reflective writing moving from description to deeper levels of reflection. The stages begin with being general at the descriptive level and increasingly move towards the specific, with varying levels of reflection and critical reflection. In the following section, we will explore the characteristics of the types of writing and give some examples of each. The learning experience is based on a student's reflections of participation in a seminar group at the beginning of their degree.

Descriptive writing tells a story. It describes an experience or situation and contains little, if any reflection. It often presents a sequence of events or activities with a general overview and doesn't focus on details or particular issues.

> *Today I went to my seminar as usual, but something felt different today. The seminar was about the social construction of childhood and I found it really interesting. I always find the topics interesting but I've been annoyed with myself recently because I haven't really spoken in seminars. I want to but when I go to put my hand up, or say something nothing happens. I'm OK talking in a smaller group but I seem to get so nervous when it's a discussion with the whole seminar. However, today I'm happy because I actually spoke and made a point in the seminar. When I was doing the preparatory reading at home I had made some notes about my own childhood and I felt confident I could say something. However, I was still really nervous before speaking – my mouth went really dry and my voice started to wobble. I hate it when it does that!*

A *descriptive account with some reflection* is more developed than the story presented in the descriptive writing. Although Moon (2010) suggests this type of writing is still a 'basic account' (p. 215) there is more focus on the event or experience being highlighted with evidence of critical thought. For example, the writer may question what happens in the account but there are no responses to these, nor consideration of other people's perspectives or viewpoints.

> *Today the seminar was on the social construction of childhood. I find this topic really interesting and when I was doing the preparatory reading in advance I know that I wanted to say something. I'm not sure why, but it just felt right. So I made some notes and went to the seminar feeling more prepared. I was still nervous but I did it, I spoke in the seminar and made a contribution to the whole class discussion. I just wish my mouth didn't go so dry and my voice didn't wobble. I now know that it's not so bad talking in the seminar but that I still need to work on my communication and confidence skills.*

In reflective writing, there is evidence of the writer 'standing back' and thinking about the event or experience. In addition to providing an overview, there is reflective comment in the text and the writer has asked some questions to analyse the situation, like the questions you asked in the 'reflecting on a learning experience activity' earlier in this chapter. There may also be the consideration of other people's viewpoints. Moon (2010) states the level of reflection is developed further with greater and deeper level questioning and critical awareness of the individual and the reflective process.

> *I'm writing this at home after my day at the university. It happened earlier today, early this afternoon. It's now five weeks into my BA Education course and the seminar today was all about the social construction of childhood. Something that I've been wanting to do, challenging myself to do for the previous weeks is to participate in a whole seminar group discussion as I've not made any contributions yet. I'm OK talking to the people that I seem to work with regularly on smaller group tasks. I think that's because we're friends now, or becoming friends and I see them in the lectures and sometimes outside of the course. I know that they 'get me' but I've been worried about talking in the big seminar group. I think it's because I don't know the other people that well yet maybe? When I was reading my preparatory reading for the seminar this week I found it really interesting and made lots of detailed notes about the reading and also my experiences. I think these notes helped me to feel more confident in the seminar because I knew what I could say. I'm so pleased that it went quite well. People in the room nodded their heads and smiled so that was positive and it wasn't as daunting as I thought. Reflecting back, there are still things that I can do to improve e.g. my voice went wobbly and my mouth felt dry because I was nervous, I think. So this is an area that I can work on to improve. I can also talk to my seminar tutor and lecturers about developing my knowledge base through wider reading because I now understand that the more I can read around a subject, the more confident I'll be about it, and to make more contributions to the classes. It's interesting to see the change in my perspective about contributing to the seminar over the last few weeks. I think it was because I was really interested in the topic and I prepared well for the seminar. Knowing that I had read the reading, made notes on it and that I had thought about it helped. I need to continue doing this for all the seminars and to*

increase my wider reading for the other modules too. I'm also going to work on developing my confidence as I think this will help. My starting point will be the lectures on developing confidence in the Academic Development module and from there I can look up key readings and references. I'm also going to give myself more time for completing the reading and seminar tasks so that I can complete them and feel 100% on top of them.

Drawing on Moon's (2010) framework for reflective writing, we can see how the student's writing becomes more reflective. In the first example text there is some reference to feeling nervous and a lot of emotion. The writing is very tied up with the ways in which the student felt about the experience. In the second example we can see some links to critical thought – for example, they mention that they need to work on their communication and confidence skills but not discussion of how this can be achieved. In the final text example we can see that there's a lot more detail about the event and the student is 'standing back' from the situation. She's recalling in the reflection but also extending this to think about what she has learned and to think critically about her next steps in developing her communication and confidence skills to be able to contribute more to whole seminar group discussions.

Validating and linking personal experiences to literature

Reflecting on your personal experiences demonstrates your ability to analyse these, and providing anecdotes of your experiences can help you to analyse the links between educational theory and practice. You can also use it as 'evidence' to support the points you're making in building your argument. It can help you to demonstrate your knowledge and understanding of linking reality to theories in the literature. As we've mentioned in the previous section, it is important to link your personal experience anecdotes with relevant literature as this will underpin your experiences, locate them within the wider context of educational research and strengthen your arguments. In the following sections, we will consider the style and tone that you can use in your writing when you draw on your own experiences to avoid the slippery slope of conversational language when you write about yourself, and how you can link them to the literature in a meaningful way to build and strengthen your discussion.

Writing appropriately using your personal experiences: style and tone, avoiding the slippery slope of conversation when writing about yourself

When you include anecdotes about your personal experiences in assignments it is important that you appropriately draw on them and relevant literature to support your points. Owing to the personal nature of including experiences that are individual to us, those that invoke memories, thoughts and feelings when we remember and reflect on them, there is a danger that writers slip into descriptive writing. For example:

When I was younger I used to really enjoy Mathematics. Well, I remember this was until Year 3 when my teacher, who happened to also be the Head Teacher in the school said in front of everyone in the class that I wasn't very good at Maths. When I told him 'I can't do it' he turned to the whole class and said it's because I'm not very good and 'can't means won't' so I'd never be good enough. Then this had a negative effect on me and I've hated Maths ever since. I just remember crying and wanting to go home. Then I thought I'd never get anywhere in life because you need to be good at Mathematics.

This experience has clearly had a profound impact on the writer and the heightened emotion is still apparent within the text. However, within assignment writing the style and tone of reflections about personal experiences should still be academic (please see Chapters 7, 8 and 9). It is possible to outline a context with a more academic tone. The following extract draws on the same experience of a Mathematics class but the tone is academic and less emotional:

Reflecting on school, I used to enjoy Mathematics. However, when I was in Year 3 my teacher, in front of the whole class, told me that I wasn't very good at it and that I never would be because of my 'I can't do it' attitude. At the time this really upset me and it has affected my perspective about my Maths ability.

In this shorter example of an anecdote, the context is provided (e.g. reflecting upon schooling) and the writer has described the situation and the impact that it has had on her but without all of the emotional description. This helps to strengthen the academic tone of the writing.

Avoiding phrases that include your 'thoughts' and 'beliefs' will also help to strengthen the academic tone of your writing. Although you're drawing on your personal experiences, you are presenting these as part of your critical discussion to build your academic argument, and your thoughts and beliefs are one aspect of this process. In addition to these, you are presenting relevant literature and so together they create an argument which is stronger than your thoughts or beliefs in your academic writing. Using phrases such as 'I think' or 'I believe' will signal to the reader that these are weaker than an argument. Instead, you can use phrases such as 'Drawing on my reflections of the Mathematics class I would argue ...'. You're probably now thinking, 'Can I use "I" in my writing?' and we will discuss this in the following section.

Can I use 'I'?

Students often arrive at university with preconceptions about what their course will be like. For example, students often make comments that they've been told 'to never use "I" in academic writing. These ideas about academic writing and what support will be available from their lecturers and tutors are often the result of what people have heard from others' experiences or what they've learnt from the media, society and popular culture. For example, Westrup (2009, p. 21) reported that some first-year students were anxious about writing essays at university because they thought they would have 'to do it all on [their] own and it's a much higher level'. Others felt that they had to be independent from day one: 'it's about independence and learning rather than being given it [the information]'. Farhat and colleagues (2017) have also noted similar student experiences due to the contrasting change of approach to learning from guided learning to a more self- directed independent one. The first thing is to reassure you that university lecturers do not expect you to be solely independent from the beginning of your course! Being able to work independently, but also with support and guidance from your lecturers and tutors, is something that you will develop over the duration of your course. Your lecturers and resources such as this book will help you to develop the necessary skills to be an independent learner and to make decisions about your learning.

Using 'I' in your writing is another example of this. There are some written assignments where you should avoid using 'I', for example when writing an Educational Psychology report, as this is a particular genre of writing often borrowed from Science disciplines where 'I' isn't used in report writing. However, when you are drawing on your own personal experiences or writing a reflective piece, using 'I' may help you to illustrate your passion and interest in a topic and illustrate a point that you are making. It also strengthens the flow of your writing as using words and phrases such as 'the writer argues' or 'drawing on the author's experiences' can disrupt writing. With the support and guidance of your lecturers and tutors you will develop confidence in your ability to judge when using 'I' is appropriate. Each course will have different preferences, so make sure that you ask your lecturers what is required on your course.

How to link personal experiences to the literature in a meaningful way and build discussion

Linking personal experiences to the literature in a meaningful way is central to using them in your academic writing. As well as helping to demonstrate a point or explain a situation they can demonstrate your understanding of the link between theory (literature) and practice (reality) in your work. Therefore, it is important to embed your anecdotes in an effective way.

When drawing on anecdotes of your personal experiences it is important to always contextualise them with relevant literature. They should be brief and summarise an event or situation that you have encountered. In Box 11.1 we offer some guidance about how you can link the experiences to the literature.

Box 11.1   Linking personal experiences to the literature in a meaningful way and building discussion

1   Make a point and contextualise within relevant literature

The main point sets up the paragraph. It tells the reader what the writing is focusing on.

2   Write about personal experience

Summarise the experience and explain to the reader *how* it is relevant to the assignment argument. This can also clarify the idea and give the reader some concrete examples about the theory and/or concept in relation to practice/reality.

3   Analyse experience and make links from your experience to relevant literature

Links should be made between the personal experience and the literature. For example, is the experience similar to or different from that written about in the literature? If there are differences, why is this? What does other literature say? This helps to build up the discussion. Here are some useful questions to ask yourself:

- Is my experience/view similar to others?
- What are the views of others? Wider reading can help with this.
- How and in what ways are my experiences/views similar to or different from others?
- What influences these viewpoints? For example, backgrounds, policies and legislation.

4   Next step(s): implications and/or personal development – what changes can be made?

Once you have analysed your experience and linked it to the literature you can then extend the paragraph and your argument by considering 'so what?' What have you learned from looking at the interplay between your experiences and the literature? This could be in relation to your own personal development or any implications for future practices and should link to your discussion in step 3. Similarly to step 3, these should be grounded within literature. The final sentence of the paragraph should tie the paragraph and ideas together before moving on to the next paragraph or conclusion.

The following example illustrates how you can embed personal experiences within your writing and use relevant literature to build the discussion. The example is about a first-year student's reflection of their experiences of academic writing following the transition to university:

Essay writing at university has received a lot of attention from researchers; it's not just me that has been thinking about it. Since undertaking the transition to university, I have been thinking a lot about my writing and whether I'm good enough to write essays at university. It is important to be able to write essays because as Lea (1998) highlighted, summative assessments are usually based on a written assignment. Similarly, Sommerville and Crème (2005) have pointed out that success in higher education is inextricably entwined with learning and knowledge construction demonstrated in academic writing. Due to not doing as well as I expected in my A-Levels I'm worried that I will not be as good as the other students. I feel like the work that I did at college did not really help prepare me for university study. My experiences are similar to those reported in Academic Literacies research studies. For example, Lowe and Cook (2003) reported that some students experience difficulties with writing at a university standard because they are not sufficiently prepared for it. Ivanic and Simpson (1992), Lillis and Turner (2001) and Lillis (2006) also argue that academic writing at university excludes some learners because it is situated within different historical and cultural contexts shaped by dominant rules that many students are unfamiliar with. Arguably, this has implications for the transition to Higher Education and the support that students are given following the transition. In the next section I will explore some practical strategies to support students.

As you can see, the student writer has reflected on their experiences of the transition to university and how they've been feeling about writing. To strengthen this within their academic writing, they have then found a number of sources of literature to contextualise their experiences.

Chapter summary: useful points for you to implement

- Remember to reflect on your personal experiences within educational settings and environments to document your journey and thought process(es).
- Reflections on your own experiences do have value within your academic writing. Remember to find out which assignments you can include your experiences and anecdotes in.
- When using anecdotes in your writing make sure that you go beyond describing the experience and analyse it and consider any implications for practice.
- Make sure you contextualise and underpin your anecdotes with links to relevant literature. This will help you to build your discussion and argument(s).

Answers to Activity 11.1

Some of your answers might have included the following reasons or ideas:

- To help us to step back and learn from our experiences.
- To consolidate information and knowledge with a particular experience or set of experiences.
- To gain a greater awareness of ourselves and our responses to situations and other people within and around them.
- To help us understand why we do what we do and evaluate the effectiveness of this.
- To be able to identify areas that we need to improve on and critically think about how we can do this.

Reflecting on Observed Experiences in Practice

Within most educational systems and processes observation of the teaching and learning process has become commonplace. For students of Education, whether your goal is to become a teacher or not, there is perhaps no greater an insightful opportunity than the privilege of observing another educator at work. Most Education programmes incorporate an opportunity for students to spend time in an educational setting not only to provide valuable experience in a sector where they may ultimately be employed in the future, but crucially, to learn the skills of reflection and analysis upon observed experiences.

This chapter will:

- Introduce you to some of the key issues you will encounter while undertaking the role of an observer.
- Give guidance and examples of how to record observations.
- Highlight key actions and precautions you should take to ensure your observations are ethical.
- Discuss and demonstrate how to use your observations in written work.

A student's perspective: First-year placement

My placement has made up my mind that teaching is for me! It is the highlight of my week and the teachers and children make me feel so welcome. It gives me confidence that I can achieve my dream.

Different kinds of observation and their purpose

Beginning to read about classroom observation can be daunting and a little confusing. Take, for example, Wragg's presentation of the different kinds of observation that may be occurring within the education system at any one time:

a primary teacher is being observed by the school's language co-ordinator, who comes for the morning to look at what can be done in response to concern about the relatively low literacy levels of certain boys in the school;

a secondary science teacher is watched by the head of department during a one and a half hour laboratory session as part of the science department's self-appraisal exercise; a student on teaching practice is seen by a supervising teacher or tutor; a maths lesson is scrutinised by an inspector during a formal inspection of the school; a class of 7 year olds is observed by a teacher who is also a textbook writer preparing a series of mathematics activities for young children; a researcher studying teachers' questioning techniques watches a secondary geography class, noting down the various questions asked by the teacher and the responses obtained. (Wragg, 1999, p. 3)

From this quote, the myriad of different reasons as to why an observation may take place becomes apparent. In terms of observational opportunities within an Education programme, these might entail:

- A group trip to observe teaching in a particular environment to learn more about a specific style or approach – for example, visiting a Montessori school.
- A small-scale piece of primary research as part of a dissertation or final project – for example, you decide you'd like to undertake research about the experiences of newly qualified teachers in their first term and undertake observations and interviews with them.
- A placement in a setting, whereby you take on the role of observer – for example, you might be recording instances of particular language used in the classroom that could be reinforcing gender stereotypes.
- Time spent in a setting where you are supporting teaching, but also keeping a reflective journal – for example, your role is one of a voluntary teaching assistant, and you are keeping notes about the dynamics of pupil friendships.
- A data gathering exercise to inform your focus within a project – for example, visiting a further education college and undertaking observations with adult learners to pursue a project that compares the teaching of vocational subjects to academic studies.

As with Wragg's examples above, each of these instances involve some kind of observation but for very different *purposes,* and it is crucial that you are certain about the purpose of your time spent as an educational observer, to make sure you can record and write about this correctly.

The beauty of observation is that through being fortunate enough to be granted access into the domain of another educator, we can notice all manner of aspects of the teaching and learning process that bypass us when we are in the role of pupil or student ourselves, or expressed otherwise: 'Observation is used in education if the purpose is to capture something of the dynamics and complexities of particular activities and events as they unfold right before your very eyes' (Sharp, 2009, p. 83). Observation is also a useful method of data collection alongside another tool such as interviews or questionnaires, as often the perceptions or experiences of an event supplied by someone when asked may in fact appear to be very different when observed.

The two main kinds of observational approaches that you might encounter are referred to as either *participant* observation, or *non-participant* observation:

Participant observation

Put simply, this kind of observation describes a scenario where you are joining in with those you are observing – for example, sitting at a table alongside learners and having discussions with them or supporting their learning.

Non-participant observation

Being a non-participant observer requires separation from the teaching and learning activities and taking more of a detached role – for example, sitting at the back of a classroom to observe, but not participating in the class.

Each approach differs, and is more or less appropriate depending on the purpose of your observations. As a participant observer you will get a more 'authentic' experience by joining in, truly becoming immersed in the environment and with the learners, and therefore get first-hand experience of learning in that context. However, it is more challenging to keep a record (i.e. notes of your observations, sometimes referred to as 'field notes') when you are also one of the learners. Being a non-participant observer does lend itself more appropriately to recording events and observations from a detached and objective perspective, and is usually the only approach you can take if you're planning to undertake some form of structured observation (as referred to in the final row of Table 12.1).

What exactly is being observed?

What you actually record as your observations will vary. Let's take some of the examples given above and consider what you might actually be recording, writing down or taking away as 'evidence' of observations. In some of the instances given you might be collecting a range of data types, which would be referred to as 'mixed methods' (Table 12.1).

Table 12.1   The nature of observations in different settings

Type of setting and observation	Kind of observational record produced
A group trip to observe teaching in a particular environment to learn more about a specific style or approach, e.g. visiting a Montessori school	Images of the classroom (see section on ethics) Reflective notes on some classes as a participant observer, reflective notes following conversations with teachers
A small-scale piece of primary research as part of a dissertation or final project, e.g. you decide you'd like to undertake research about the experiences of newly qualified teachers (NQTs) in their first term and undertake observations and interviews with them	Interview transcripts after recoded interviews with NQTs Written text in a notebook where you recorded your reflections from the back of a classroom as a non-participant observer

Type of setting and observation	Kind of observational record produced
A placement in a setting, whereby you take on the role of observer, e.g. you might be recording instances of particular language used in the classroom that could be reinforcing gender stereotypes	A structured grid marked with ticks you added every time teachers used a gender-specific term during class, e.g. 'good girl', 'good lad'. A structured grid marked with ticks to record how many times girls were picked when they put their hands up to answer, and how many times boys were picked.

You may be given specific templates to use for recording observations as part of your module or course or you may be asked to create one yourself. The section later in the chapter entitled 'Recording your observations' considers ways of recording and then writing up your observations.

Ethical issues in observation

Carrying out observations or gathering data in any kind of educational context (e.g. questionnaires with teachers or focus groups with pupils) requires careful and systematic consideration of ethical procedures. Your course tutors and institution will have specific requirements in terms of their ethical guidelines (e.g. an ethical checklist you may be required to complete), and it is essential that you adhere to what is required of you. Fulfilling any ethical requirements or submitting paperwork is usually a prerequisite to any research or data gathering you may wish to do as part of your degree programme. However, ethics should not be perceived purely as a box-ticking exercise; taking an ethical approach in your observations is something that should influence your planning, data gathering, analysis and write-up of observational practice from start to finish.

In its most simple sense, ethics is about protecting individuals from harm or deception; this includes both those who are involved in your observations or research *and yourself*. The British Educational Research Association (BERA) in their *Ethical Guidelines for Educational Research* document stress that:

> educational researchers should operate within an ethic of respect for any persons involved in the research they are undertaking. Individuals should be treated fairly, sensitively, with dignity, and within an ethic of respect and freedom from prejudice regardless of age, gender, sexuality, race, ethnicity, class, nationality, cultural identity, partnership status, faith, disability, political belief or any other significant difference. This ethic of respect should apply to both the researchers themselves and any individuals participating in the research either directly or indirectly. (2011, p. 5)

It is impossible to give a comprehensive and detailed overview of all the specific ethical precautions or actions researchers should undertake within this chapter, but below is a list of key issues for consideration, along with some suggested actions.

Access – How you gain access to your educational setting may vary. What's important to bear in mind here is that you are open and transparent about the purpose of your intended observations, and that the setting in no way feels coerced to accept you as a student observer. So, communications and initial enquires with your setting (e.g. an email to the school) should make it clear what you are asking of them (e.g. an opportunity to observe History classes one morning per week for 8 weeks) and why (e.g. giving an overview of your degree programme, the requirements of that particular module or course, contact details of relevant tutors and also details about Disclosure and Barring Service [criminal record] checks or health and safety information, as per your university's guidance).

Informed consent – Anyone about whom you are gathering data should be aware of this, and have consented to it – or had the opportunity to *not* be included in this data gathering. This, however, can be somewhat tricky in an observational setting as consent (i.e. permission) to be in the classroom and recording data about the participants will have been given by teachers or head teachers who have permitted you to undertake observations in that classroom. It is quite possible that the learners have had no say or option to 'opt out' of your data collection. However, it is possible to behave in a conscientious and ethical manner yourself, by observing and looking closely for indications where pupils may be wary or uncomfortable with an adult watching them closely, or if it is apparent that they are self-conscious with the idea of an adult clearly writing down things about them. In any such instances, it is your own individual responsibility to either abstain from collecting data or have a conversation with the pupils yourself to explain the purpose of your records, and ask them if they are happy for you to write about them anonymously. In seeking permission in this way you also need to consider the learners' competence, that is, do they truly understand what you are asking them? This is particularly important with very young pupils or with learners who may have learning difficulties.

Confidentiality and privacy – Remember that as an observer being granted access to educational events, opportunities and journeys you are in a privileged position. On some occasions you may be privy to sensitive or confidential information that teachers or other professionals share with you, for example in relation to safeguarding or special educational needs. At all times you should keep this information confidential and private, ensuring you do not discuss this with people outside of the school. If the nature of your assessed work for your observations relates to sensitive or confidential information, then discuss this with your tutor and ensure that you have taken particular precautions with regard to anonymity.

Anonymity – No one participating in your research should be identifiable. Therefore, individuals who read your observations or assignment based on these observations should not be able to recognise any teachers, learners or other individuals you might refer to. In most instances, therefore, assigning pseudonyms to those you refer to will be essential to keep individuals anonymous. If you are gathering images as part of your data (e.g. pictures of the classroom or learners at work) then firstly you must gain permission to do this from the teacher and anyone else they advise within that setting, and secondly it is usually protocol to ensure that no learners' faces are identifiable in any images, so this might mean taking pictures from a distance with learners not facing you; blurring out faces; or taking pictures that do not feature any individuals at all, for example of the empty classroom or particular resources being used.

Representation – Aside from the points above that tend to relate to individuals, it is necessary to consider the implications of the way that you represent people, professions and educational establishments in your records and work. Firstly, bear in mind that being an observer in a classroom does not make you qualified to pass judgement upon the quality or standard of teaching, and you should take great care not to record flippant, strongly opinionated or derogatory remarks in any of your observations. Representing and making generalised statements or claims about individuals or a whole school as a result of limited observations is unfair and not the job of an undergraduate student undertaking observations. It's also worth remembering that the teacher you are observing may pass by and see what you have written in your notebook, and so to maintain your own 'professional' integrity (as a student) take care with the nature of what you record.

These principles and guidelines above not only will protect the participants that you're working with, but will also ensure you protect yourself. Your university may have more specific guidelines about the storage and destruction of data such as field notes or images, and you should adhere to these as advised.

Finally, it is important to note here that the issue of ethics in undertaking primary research is a vast and complex area, and a full understanding of this cannot by any means be contained within this chapter. We would recommend that for more extensive primary research, and to further inform discussions around ethics that you may need to reflect in assignments, you consult some of the following useful sources:

- BERA (British Educational Research Association) (2011) *Ethical Guidelines for Educational Research.* Available from: www.bera.ac.uk/wp-content/uploads/2014/02/BERA-Ethical-Guidelines-2011.pdf?noredirect=1

- Brooks, R., te Riele, K. and Maguire, M. (2014) *Ethics and Education Research.* London: SAGE Publications.

- For more in-depth debates, chap. 5, in Cohen, L., Manion, L. and Morrison, K. (2011) *Research Methods in Education.* London: Routledge.

Recording your observations

In situ, while you are observing, your notes will no doubt look rather haphazard and perhaps only legible to yourself. It's usually best to use a small notebook (perhaps around A5 size), especially if you are a participant observer as you can then pick it up easily and carry it around with you.

For each new entry, or session, be sure to start a new page, or draw a line across, and then record basic details at the top such as: Date and time; Class; Subject/Lesson; Name of teacher; and any other necessary details – for example, supply teacher, new pupils, etc.

Example 12.1   Written observation

Date and time: Tuesday 12th September, 10am   Class: Year 7
Subject/Lesson: History: Life of Julius Caesar   Name of teacher: Mrs Jones

- Class enters noisily and takes some time to settle down. One group of girls at the back carry on talking and Mrs Jones has to interrupt them to begin class; it takes them a few minutes to settle down and this takes up 3–4 minutes at the beginning of the class.
- Teacher takes time to look around room and ask pupils how they are; she tries to make eye contact with all of them to make a connection.
- Class starts with discussions about homework that students had undertaken online, and some feedback on this. About half of the class take some notes based on this feedback. One pupil asked a related question. The rest of the pupils don't seem bothered about the feedback.
- Teacher introduces topic of Julius Caesar and displays aims of the lesson on the board. Pupils seem to zone out a bit here.
- Starts by asking pupils in pairs to write down three things they know about Julius Caesar – crediting the pupils with what they already know seems to work well with some pupils. Some of the more able pupils seem to be racing to write down everything they can (more than 3), others seem pretty despondent, looking up at ceiling, long 'Ermm' and don't get anything written down. The one pupil with a Teaching Assistant (TA) next to him seems quite unaffected by distractions in the room and focuses well on working with his TA to get ideas down on paper. However, the pupils sitting around him clearly eavesdrop on his conversations with the TA and this seems to be somewhat of a distraction for them.
- Teacher brings class back together and takes these ideas and creates spider diagram on whiteboard. She takes care to try and pick from a range of pupils in the group. Some are reluctant to give their ideas, seem to be lacking in confidence or don't want to be heard talking in front of their peers.
- Teacher shows a number of different images of Caesar (e.g. paintings, statutes) and asks pupils what kind of man they think he was based on these depictions. This seems to involve more of the class, and some of those who struggled to write answers to the first question have lots of contributions. She is good at turning slightly silly answers into an opportunity for discussion, e.g. 'Why has he got leaves on his head?', explaining the significance and meaning of the laurel crown. These images are a good way to get some of the class who haven't contributed to talk.
- The class is shown a 6-minute animation about Caesar – this has some comedy in it so is very well received. Every single pupil is engaged and watches it very attentively. One or two pupils write some things down. She then asks them what they can add to their list they made at the beginning of class and goes around the room listening and encouraging the pupils in their discussions. This strategy stops the same group of girls (talking before) going off on a tangent.
- Teacher draws class to a close and points out homework to pupils online.

Example 12.2　Structured quantitative observation

Date and time:　Tuesday 12th September, 10am　　Class: Year 7
Subject/Lesson:　History: Life of Julius Caesar　　Name of teacher: Mrs Jones

Event/Observation	Number of times observed	Notes
1. Teacher praise	卌 II	More enthusiastic to boys than girls
2. Teacher reprimand	卌	Often to same pupils
3. Teacher encouragement	卌 卌 III	
4. Teacher prompting recall of information	II	
5. Teacher uses ideas of pupils	IIII	Does this skilfully
6. Teacher poses question	卌 卌 II	Sometimes has to rephrase to elicit response
7. Teacher gives instructions	卌 卌 卌 I	
8. Pupil contributions (invited/ requested)	卌 卌 卌 卌 I	
9. Pupil contributions (uninvited)	III	
10. Pupil interruptions	IIII	Generally constitute talking (off topic)

As can be seen from the examples above, these records translate what is being observed into either qualitative (usually written) or quantitative (numerical) data. Each one of these examples has advantages and disadvantages, for example the second example would allow you to make descriptive statements about the frequency of interactions or events in the classroom. This would be useful if your focus is upon some aspect of pedagogical practice, such as observing the implementation of behaviouristic strategies or approaches. In contrast, the first qualitative example would allow you to obtain and reflect upon richer data that depicts an environment, context and not just what had happened, or *how* often, but to begin to consider *why* certain interactions have occurred, and what the consequences of these might be.

A common query from students undertaking observational work in educational setting is, 'What should I be writing down?' Be reassured, firstly, that taking field notes as part of observational practice is a skill that develops, and it's perfectly normal to emerge from your first observation with pages and pages of notes, which then become more refined and concise over the coming weeks and months. It is also worth bearing in mind that it's better to have a few too many notes that you can then edit down, as opposed to too few notes.

TIPS FOR RECORDING OBSERVATIONS

Don't rely on your memory and tell yourself 'I'll write that down later'. Do it then and there!

Make it a habit to 'write up' your notes after each observation. Ensure they are legible (i.e. rewritten or typed up), organised (i.e. dated, filed away) and also take the time to add a few reflections in addition to just recording the events. For example, you might note down changes you've observed over a few weeks, something that particularly struck you, your reflections on an issue you discussed with the teacher and so on. These reflections are like gold dust in an observational sense, and if you neglect to record them then you'll struggle to retrieve these thoughts and engage with them again.

ACTIVITY 12.1

Identifying what to note in your observations

Type 'classroom observations' into YouTube. Be aware that among the videos that will appear, there is a large variation in quality, purpose, focus, editing and relevance. Browse through a couple and begin to consider what kinds of notes you might make if you were an observer in these contexts. Some useful questions to pose include:

- What is the teacher doing?
- What are the learners doing?
- Are there any notable features of the classroom environment? Does the environment (e.g. layout) seem significant?
- In what ways does the teacher pick up on unspoken communication?
- What kinds of communication occurs between the learners?
- Are there other adults in the room (e.g. teaching assistants), and what is their role?
- Do the learners seem more or less engaged at certain times? How can you tell?
- Do some resources and activities seem to capture the attention of learners more than others?
- Do learners stay 'on task'? If not, why not? Do some learners seem better at staying on task than others?
- What actions does the teacher take to differentiate or individualise the learning to particular learners and their specific needs?
- Is the body language of the teacher significant?
- Do you need to record any images such as a map/plan of the room or take pictures of work produced or resources used? (see the discussion on ethics earlier in this chapter for points about use of images).

The kind of data you require and the depth of this will depend very much on the purpose of your observation, your role and assignments linked to your time in educational settings. You will find many different kinds of templates and examples of classroom observations if you search for a sample on the internet, but do be sure to adhere to guidance given to you by your tutors.

How to use your observations in your written work

The next steps in thinking about educational observations is what to do with them once your data collection is complete. Your module, or course, may have very specific guidance about the kinds of observations or data to include. Some may require evidence of your observations (which may be referred to as diaries, journal entries or field notes) in full in an appendix to an assessed piece of work, others may require summarised reflections.

Whatever form you will present them in, embedding your observations and reflections in your written work can be challenging. The main reasons students can struggle with including personal observations and reflections in written work tend to be:

- Lack of student confidence in the value of what they have written and recorded.
- Nervousness around ethical issues.
- Uncertainty about how to integrate comments and data that may be recorded in the first person into an 'academic' piece of work.

Each of these concerns can be addressed if you take care to approach your observational writing with planning and consideration.

Firstly, **lack of confidence** in what you might have recorded. It is important not to belittle or devalue your observations; they are a valid and credible record of what *you* observed, at that time, in that space, on that day. A balanced approach is vital here; we do need to recognise that our observations have limitations dependent upon time, context and place, and that they are certainly not representative of *all* kinds of educational settings, classrooms or pedagogical interactions. There's also a significant part of ourselves that we bring to our observations in the way of what we choose to record (or omit), and our interpretation of our observations – bear in mind that someone else's observations might look very different to yours. However, the field notes, diary or journal you have created is a valuable piece of educational data, and provided you recognise its limitations and use if appropriately, you should try to feel proud of your observations and use them in a meaningful way.

Understandably, some students feel anxious about the way they use observations because of **ethical concerns**. You are right to be mindful of this, and to take every possible action to be conscientious about the way you record and report upon your observations. Provided you follow the guidance from your institution/tutors, and take the points in the previous section into consideration, you will be acting in an ethical manner. Take the time to read around the recommended resources to learn more about ethical practice as an educational researcher.

Lastly, it can be challenging to **integrate your own observations into written work**, and so this chapter ends by spending some time looking at ways to achieve this.

A common difficulty experienced here by students can be due to a shift in writing style, as often a majority of assignments require a formal, traditional academic approach which precludes anything written in the first person (i.e. using 'I'). Shaking off the habit of writing in the third person can be difficult to do, but an important skill to develop for Education students is the ability to shift writing styles in accordance with what is required.

Chapter 11 has given you a good deal of ideas about writing reflectively around your *own* educational experiences, and indeed many of the principles and approaches highlighted also apply when you are writing about observational experiences. Below are some overall pointers to take into account when approaching an assignment task that requires you to integrate your observations, followed by an excerpt of an example discussion that blends evidence from observations and wider literature.

1 Firstly, take care to be selective about what you include from your observations. It's likely that you will be asked to present your full observations (e.g. a diary or field notes) as an appendix to a written assignment, which means that the parts of your observations you include in your actual assignment will be heavily edited and must be directly relevant to the issues you are discussing. Just as there is little value (and few marks to be gained) in reproducing very extensive passages of text from a book within your assignment, the same usually applies to your observational records. You must look through your observations and choose the most relevant and concise account of a particular event, conversation or observation and represent this in your assignment appropriately. If, for example, you are writing a discussion around the use of behaviour strategies that you observed being implemented, then only refer to very specific instances of your observations that directly relate to and support what you are discussing.

2 Secondly, remember that using evidence and examples from your observations is akin to having another source of evidence in addition to literature, and you should seek to balance and blend the way you use both of these. This means that when we discuss a point relevant to our observations, to expand upon and make our discussions credible we need to refer to both examples from observations, and published literature, ultimately trying to establish the extent to which what we have observed in practice is reflected in the literature (or not).

3 Thirdly, maintaining an appropriate style and tone when introducing your own observations will help you to integrate and blend evidence from both published texts and observations. This means you need to take a consistent approach in the way you refer to what you have recorded, use of the first person and taking care to avoid slipping into a conversational tone.

Example: excerpt from a discussion about observed experiences

One area that I became particularly interested in during my time with the year 6 class was the teacher's use of alternative strategies to communicate with two pupils who are on the autistic spectrum, Zach and Jacob*. Both boys generally work well within the classroom, applying themselves quite diligently to tasks set with the support of a full time teaching assistant (TA) who is assigned to work with both of them.

Prior to my observations at Mount Green Primary*, I had not considered in any detail the practicalities of including pupils with ASD into day to day teaching, but from the very start of my observations I noticed a number of different strategies and tools used by the teacher, the TA, and even fellow pupils to make communication with Zach and Jacob more effective, and to improve social communication and friendships with their peers. This can be problematic for many learners with ASD, as recognised by Humphrey and Symes (2010) and Rowley et al. (2012) who found that pupils with Autism are more likely to experience social exclusion and have a lack of social support. I certainly noted in my observations during break times that Zach and Jacob tended to interact predominantly with one another, or with no one else at all, and spend a significant amount of their free time engaged in individual activities. Those I recorded in particular were frequent instances of sitting on the friendship bench alone, and repeatedly working with the large blocks in the playground and excluding others from participating (see diaries dated 13th February, 27th February and 6th March).

Mrs Vickerstaff*, the class teacher, explained to me that I would observe some strategies used to help Zach and Jacob communicate better in the classroom, and the first of these I noticed from the outset was the use of PECS (Picture Exchange System), a language programme using symbols and signs that helps some pupils to express their feelings and preferences, and can be especially valuable as it allows them to communicate spontaneously rather than always being asked by an adult (Magiati and Howlin, 2003). I observed that the PECS system that was made available to Zach and Jacob was in the form of personalised books for each of them, full of symbols and relevant pictures. I was informed by the TA that they were both at different stages of using PECs (there is a six stage programme), and that Jacob seemed to be progressing faster in his use of the symbols, I noted this on several occasions in my observations, in particular during sessions where the class was given an element of free choice and independent tasks, as can be seen in the observation below:

> During the library session where pupils had free choice to select books, there was a 10-minute time limit set for pupils to select a book and then settle down for independent reading. Zach worked with the TA closely to find a specific book he often chose, whereas in contrast Jacob, although hesitant at first, used his PECs symbols to indicate to Mrs Vickerstaff when he wanted to select a different book, by choosing the symbol in his book and spontaneously taking this over to her to indicate he wanted a book swap. (6th February, 2pm class)

This example illustrated to me the effectiveness of using pictures and symbols for communication, a method which has been increasingly recognised through both the use of PECs (Magiati and Howli, 2003; Webb, 2000) and also the use of social stories, a combination of words and simple pictures described as a 'meaningful, patient, non-judgemental, respectful and reassuring description of life' (Timmins, 2017, p. 17). See Appendix 2 for some images of social story boards and pages from Jacob's PECs book, pictures that he allowed me to take with permission.

*note these are pseudonyms

This excerpt illustrates the balance and blend between individual observations and evidence gained as a result of research from relevant literature. In effect, a straightforward way to think about integrating observations into your work is simply to consider them as another piece of literature, or evidence that you can cite and refer to in order to add greater depth, weight and a variety of perspectives to your discussions. Balancing your use of literature and observations will add a richness to not only the assignments you produce, but your own reflections and understanding of the realities of the educational processes. It seems particularly apt to end this chapter with a relevant quotation from the late Ted Wragg, whose books on classroom observation are still of great value and much used by students undertaking observation:

> despite some of the difficulties of visiting classrooms and observing lessons, it is still a worthwhile enterprise and one that should be undertaken in a thoughtful and professional manner. There is still a great deal to be learned by any teacher, novice or seasoned practitioner, or by any investigator. Good classroom observation can lie at the heart of both understanding professional practice and improving its quality. (Wragg, 1999, p. 17)

Chapter summary: useful points for you to implement

- Be very aware that the nature of your written observations and how you will report upon these can vary significantly depending on the purpose of your presence in an educational setting and what assignment tasks you have been set.
- Take great care to reliably and meticulously record details of your observations, ensure they are legible and store them in a safe and organised manner.
- Take your responsibility as an educational researcher seriously, and reflect ethical considerations and principles in your written work.

Next Steps: Taking Your Education Degree Forward

Whatever stage you're at in your studies, this chapter is one to read when you're at a point to engage in reflection about the value of your degree beyond your time at university. It's never too early to start thinking about your life after graduation, and if you do give your post-graduation plans some thought early on, this will enable you to take advantage of various opportunities throughout your degree that will help to enhance your employability, or make you a stronger candidate for further study or training. This chapter will:

- Look at what Education graduates do.
- Help you to reflect upon what you have learned about your subject and yourself during your studies; your strengths; and areas that can be developed further.
- Help you to consider the experiences you've had and identify transferable skills you're developing/have developed for employment and/or further study.

What do Education graduates do?

It's true that the majority of Education graduates progress to postgraduate teacher training, or careers supporting teaching and learning in some way. If the course you are undertaking already leads to qualified teacher status (e.g. a B.Ed., or BA in Primary Education) then the need to undertake postgraduate training will not apply to you, and the latter contents of this chapter will be more relevant.

For graduates of an Education-related degree who wish to progress to teacher training, firstly this section will briefly consider teaching options and routes. However, not all Education graduates intend to or go on to teach, and so we will then look at a number of different routes that might be of interest.

Moving on to teach

Currently in the UK, teaching is a graduate-led profession, which means that anyone wanting to undertake comprehensive Initial Teacher Education (ITE, i.e. teacher training) needs a degree in nearly all instances; the exception to this is some independent (private) schools, free schools or academies, although this is not very common.

Remember that there may be more sectors or kinds of institutions to teach in than you think:

- Early years (generally under 5s)
- Primary (approx. 4–11 years)
- Secondary (11–16)
- Further, or Post-Compulsory (over 16s and adults)
- Higher Education (i.e. university)

In addition, other educational establishments that you might wish to teach in include Pupil Referral Units, Special Schools, Prisons or adult training providers.

Teacher training providers have their own admissions criteria that can differ from place to place (a little like universities), but current provision specifies that there are two key routes into teacher training:

University-led training, which involves going to study for another year and combining time learning at university with time in a school placement to gain a Postgraduate Certificate in Education (PGCE) or a Postgraduate Diploma in Education (PGDE) in Scotland. School-led training, which involves training 'on the job' within a school, often in partnership with a local university.

Routes and requirements vary and can be subject to change according to government policy, so always check the most up-to-date information, which can be found by simply searching online for:

- 'Get into Teaching' if you're in England
- 'Teacher training and education in Wales' if you're in Wales
- 'Teach in Scotland' if you're in Scotland
- 'Initial teacher education' if you're in Northern Ireland.

You should bear in mind at an early stage of your studies that what you do as part of your degree can have a significant impact upon the teaching options open to you. For example, if you want to teach in secondary education, then for the most part it is usually expected that at least half of your degree is in the curriculum subject you wish to teach, so that you are a subject specialist. So, for example, you might be combining Education with History, a Science, English or a Sports-related subject in order to teach one of these at secondary level.

An absolute expectation is that you have a good deal of experience with the kinds of learners that you aspire to work with, and so plenty of time in schools or other relevant environments will be essential to ensure you are an attractive candidate for a place on a teacher training scheme, whether it's in a university or school-based. There may be all sorts of opportunities for you to gain relevant experience:

- Placements or observations in educational settings.
- Trips to relevant places – for example, schools with contrasting educational philosophies, visits to schools overseas.
- Any kind of voluntary work with the kinds of learners you wish to work with – for example, mentoring young people in community settings, school holiday play

schemes, working with charities who provide activities for children with special educational needs and disabilities, sports coaching, supporting community groups working with families and young children and so on. Look at https://do-it.org/ and search for opportunities with relevant groups of people, or see if your university has any support available to help you find volunteering opportunities.

Non-teaching destinations and professions

In its broadest sense, an Education degree equips you with many skills that are of value to a whole range of job roles and sectors. It's usually the case that most Education graduates progress to undertake work that involves working *with* people in society in a face-to-face or supportive role, often in the public sector.

The Quality Assurance Agency (QAA) benchmarks for Education identify the following set of transferable skills such that Education graduates are able to:

- Construct and communicate oral and written arguments
- Make effective use of technology
- Interpret and present relevant numerical information
- Work effectively with others as part of a team, taking different roles
- Improve their own learning and performance, through the development of study and research skills, and a capacity to plan, manage and reflect on their own learning
- Identify, synthesise, evaluate, and analyse problems and solutions
- Respond positively and constructively to changing environments.

QAA (2015, p. 10)

These kinds of skills are of great value in any number of job roles, or for further research or study. Other related job destinations for Education graduates (some of which include further postgraduate study) include:

- Community education officer
- English as a foreign language teacher (often overseas)
- Learning mentor
- Careers advisor
- Family support worker
- Play therapist
- Youth worker
- Occupational Therapist
- Social Worker.

For much more comprehensive advice on job roles related to Education, look at the Prospects careers website: www.prospects.ac.uk/careers-advice/what-can-i-do-with-my-degree/education.

Postgraduate study

For some students, postgraduate study will be necessary to help them work towards their chosen profession, as is the case for teaching. Other relevant professions where specific postgraduate study is required include working as an Educational Psychologist, or Social Worker, both of which require further taught, postgraduate study. Again, look on the Prospects website for further detail here.

Alternatively, you may wish to continue your academic studies, progressing on to further postgraduate qualifications. Most commonly these might be a Master's (MA) or Master's by Research (MRes) of some description, or further progression on to Doctoral study – for example, a PhD. There are a vast array of possibilities here and it is essential that you spend time researching appropriate courses, institutions, and supervisors, that is, the staff who will teach on the course. The content and focus of postgraduate study often allows you to pursue a particular educational interest in greater depth, for example a Master's around International Education, Music, Policy, Early Years, Psychology or Inclusive Education. Take your time to research not only the course and the institution, but also the implications of studying for another year or two financially, *and* also be sure to ask yourself how a Master's degree will be of use to you, and what you hope to progress on to *afterwards*.

If you have really been bitten by the research bug, then you may aspire towards a career in educational or social research, and so a Master's, or even PhD route, is usually necessary. For a few fortunate students, there are a range of scholarships and bursaries available, such as those from UK Research Councils, or sometimes other smaller organisations.

For advice and information on Master's and PhD study, look at www.prospects.ac.uk/postgraduate-study or contact universities directly.

Identifying transferable skills

Transferable skills are the skills and attributes that you develop in one area that can then be transferred to another type of activity. For example, the skills learnt and developed while working part-time on the till in a grocery store – for example, meeting customers and ensuring efficient and high levels of customer service – can be applied to greeting and networking with clients or new colleagues. In addition to highlighting what skills you have, you need to be able to illustrate evidence of these.

Identifying and applying your skills for employment

As we have highlighted earlier in this chapter, there is an expectation that during your degree you will gain experience of working in a career that you're interested in pursuing post-graduation. Depending upon your interests, this may be in a teaching role, working in an educational setting, or other sectors – for example, within the media or a Human Resources (HR) department if you wish to move away from the education sector. Regardless of your chosen career path, the experience that you have gained while undertaking a placement, working in the voluntary sector or in paid employment, together with skills developed on your course, will help you when applying for jobs or postgraduate study.

What skills do different jobs require?

To help you begin to think about skills that are required for certain job roles, have a look at the jobs available in an area of employment that interests you. If you're not sure what's out there, have a look at https://targetjobs.co.uk/.

- What are the key characteristics identified in the job description and person specification?
- How can you demonstrate and evidence these characteristics in an application?
- Do you notice any similarities and/or differences between the job adverts?
- What knowledge and skills do you feel you need to work on and develop further?

When identifying your transferable skills, the first thing to do is reflect back on your studies and any work experience you have undertaken. As we discussed in Chapter 11, reflection helps us to understand more about ourselves and where we need to focus developments. Reflection also enables us to think about the skills we are learning, what we have learnt and how these can be applied to the career we're interested in. When thinking about what skills and attributes you have and how these link to employment it is useful to split your reflections into (1) your degree course and (2) your work experience.

1 Your degree course

You may have chosen to study an Education degree because you think you would like to have a career in teaching or working in an educational setting or because you are interested in wider issues regarding education and society more widely. The knowledge and skills that you have learnt on your course can be worked into transferable skills for employment. As part of your course there may also be opportunities to take part in extracurricular activities that can count as transferable skills. For example, students can often take part in university department or school meetings as student representatives or organisers of societies.

Identifying your course knowledge and skills

This activity will help you to identify the knowledge and skills that you have developed, or are developing, from your course.

Look back over your module notes and work and make a list of the subject-specific knowledge and skills that you have developed throughout your degree, or so far, depending on what stage you're at. Go through the list and consider whether these would be of value to employers or postgraduate courses. For example:

- In a module entitled 'Children, Special Educational Needs and Disability', a student could identify that they have subject-specific knowledge about the Special Educational Needs and Disability Code of Practice, Assessment, Safeguarding and a range of strategies to promote inclusion in schools.

- While in another module such as a policy-focused one, a student could identify a wider subject-knowledge base about understanding the relationship between society and political contexts.

The skills you develop by attending lectures, participating in seminars and completing assessments will also be transferable for employment – for example, through activities such as undertaking group work, answering questions, writing assignments and delivering presentations.

- In both courses students could identify that they have developed critical, analytical and evaluative skills through undertaking reading for assignments.

Jennifer Moon's work (2009) on academic assertiveness is useful here; in her book she identifies a number of broader (not subject-specific) situations throughout a degree programme that may be challenging and require proactive thought to help you move on and progress. These are also the kinds of situations you can reflect upon and use to identify the skills you learned, or the ways in which these experiences helped you to develop. Some of the examples she gives as challenging academic situations you might have encountered include:

- Seminars, where you are expected to contribute and talk in front of others.
- Instances where your thinking has been challenged – for example, in debates where your viewpoint is opposed.
- Times when you needed to seek out additional support or information from specialist services – for example, in relation to use of technology or study skills.
- How you felt after receiving feedback, and what you did as a result of receiving feedback.
- Situations when you had to work in a group and this was not straightforward.

Moon (2009) suggests that it is useful to reflect on such situations to think about how you managed your thoughts and feelings. She defines academic assertiveness as:

a set of emotional and psychological orientations and behaviors that enables a learner appropriately to manage the challenges to the self in the course of learning and their experiences in formal education. (p. 23)

We can take further from her work if we look at just a few of the particular behaviours Moon identifies that might be required of you during your time as a learner:

- Finding an appropriate 'voice' or form of expression through which to engage in critical thinking or debate.
- A willingness to challenge, to disagree and to seek or accept a challenge.
- The ability to cope with the likelihood of not being 'right' sometimes, making an error or failing, and making an effective recovery from these situations.
- A willingness to change one's mind if necessary (Moon, 2009, p. 23).

These are all the kinds of behaviours that you might have needed at some point in your degree programme, and if you can reflect and identify instances or situations where these behaviours were required of you, then these also become useful 'gains' you can talk about that have been developed as a result of your time studying. For example, perhaps you began your studies feeling very shy about talking in front of others, but you committed to overcoming this anxiety and you're able to talk about the shift in mindset you have had to employ, and can now demonstrate that this is an area where you've experienced significant personal development, as evidenced through the strong grades you received for a final-year presentation. Sometimes the skills and parts of ourselves that we develop through our studies are not immediately obvious, and so breaking down aspects of study into smaller situations or encounters can also be a helpful way to reflect and identify development.

2 **Your work experience**

There are many different ways that you can gain work experience during your degree course and it can take a variety of names including: placement(s); internship(s); volunteering; and employed paid work. Placements and internships may be embedded within your course and they can either be paid or unpaid. They are a great way to understand what skills and knowledge you have, how you can apply them to the work environment and what you still need to develop to enhance your employability.

A student's perspective: Second-year placement reflection

I've thoroughly enjoyed my time on placements throughout my degree because as an aspiring teacher it's one of the most important and valuable ways of gaining experience in the profession.

I've loved being able to observe a variety of teaching methods whilst also joining in as a helping hand. I've enjoyed learning about teaching theories in my degree and have benefited from talking to different teachers whilst also observing day-to-day life in schools.

Having the chance to specifically observe a lesson provides a great new insight into things you may not have picked up on when working in the classroom as a volunteer which I've valued in my placement experience.

In addition to learning about yourself, work experience can also help you to learn about the career role you're interested in, the environment and what working with colleagues may involve; it doesn't matter if the job role is totally unrelated to the Education sector, there will still be key skills that you have gained and can reflect upon. Some key questions to help understand the work environment are:

- What did you enjoy the best of the experience? Why?
- What didn't you enjoy? Why?
- Can you see your 'future self' working in a similar environment?
- What qualifications and experiences do you need to have for working in this (or a similar) role in the environment?

ACTIVITY 13.3

Identifying skills and knowledge from your work experience

This activity will help you to identify the knowledge and skills that you have developed or are developing from your work experience. Using the example below, think about how your experiences (voluntary or paid work) can help you to demonstrate the transferable skills.

Transferable skill	Experience	Further development?
Working in a team	On placement in a primary school I worked closely with the class teachers to develop learning resources for learners with additional needs.	More concrete examples needed.
Report writing		I need more experience of writing reports in the work environment. I should focus on accuracy.
Giving presentations	While working at an educational technology company I gave regular presentations. I was responsible for educating people about how the company products worked. As a result of my persuasive communication ten people placed orders.	Continue development.
Problem solving	Whilst working at a hotel as a receptionist I have to be the first point of contact for residents who have difficulties, identify and offer an appropriate solution and communicate this to them effectively.	Need to work on this in more educational scenarios that we discuss in seminars.

(Transferable skills identified from www.jobs.ac.uk)

Now think about what you could put in a table yourself

Transferable skill	Experience	Further development?

Looking to the future, we leave the last words of this book to some students who have graduated from Education degree programmes over the last few years. We hope their snippets of life a few years after graduation inspire you, and help you to look forward to the many opportunities and experiences.

Student experiences: A few years after graduation …

I have just accepted a job opportunity this morning! Since finishing my degree in Education & Psychology I went on to complete my Master's in Psychology Conversion. My ultimate goal is to eventually be a qualified Educational Psychologist however after the Master's I wanted to take a couple of years out to get some in school experience and give myself a break.

I have been working for a charity providing care during school holidays for Autistic children and children with other learning difficulties or disorders. Today I have just been offered a job at a secondary school working with the support staff to support the pupils with special educational needs within the mainstream school!

I have definitely relied on a lot of my knowledge that was learnt throughout my degree in Education & Psychology and drawn on this in real life experience in both primary schools and working with special needs children and it has proven to come in very handy in my interview for this job also!

After graduation I took 2 years out, working and did some voluntary work in Zimbabwe. Then, I did my PGCE last year. Currently, I'm teaching in Kuwait, at a British school and enjoying it a lot. It was hard adjusting to a whole different lifestyle and culture at first but it's amazing here.

I had a year out from education after completing my degree in Education & Psychology, working and volunteering. After the year out I completed my Psychology MSc & I have just landed a new job in which I can finally start to utilise my skills! I will be working as a targeted youth worker at a brand new youth centre which I am really looking forward to! I will also be completing an introduction to counselling course over the next few months, with the intention of pursuing this as a career (with children and adolescents).

I am currently working as a reception class teacher at a Primary School. It is challenging but I love it. The main thing that really helped me during my degree programme was the constructive feedback I received.

I have been working in a secondary Pupil Referral Unit since the year I graduated as a Level 3 Teaching Assistant and for the last year I have been the school's Careers Coordinator, which I love doing. The school attracts pupils with a variety of educational, emotional and medical needs and I have also had the opportunity to put into practice what I learned from my dissertation on social and emotional learning when I lead a SEAL (Social and Emotional Aspects of Learning) programme in school.

I am currently completing my PGCE Primary. Got 7 weeks to go and counting down! The assignments and modules in my degree programme were really helpful in this course and have acted as a good stepping stone to get me into teaching as I am only just learning how much I completed over the 3 years. I have referred back to my assignments loads with regard to things on placement.

Chapter summary: useful points for you to implement

- Research what students can do with an Education degree – there are many job roles in addition to being a teacher.
- Try and think about your employability at an early point in your degree. Beginning to think about it in your third year is too late.
- Get involved with as much of your course as possible and actively engage with work experience opportunities whether they are paid or unpaid.
- Reflect at regular intervals upon what skills and knowledge you're learning on your course and what transferable skills you can evidence from work experience.

References

Alexander, R. (2010) *Children, Their World, their Education: Final Report and Recommendations of the Cambridge Primary Review.* London: RoutledgeFalmer.

Bartlett, S. and Burton, D. (2012) *Introduction to Education Studies.* London: SAGE Publications.

Bloom, B., Englehart, M., Furst, E., Hill, W. and Krathwohl, D. (1956) *Taxonomy of Educational Objectives: The Classification of Educational Goals. Handbook I: Cognitive Domain.* New York and Toronto: Longmans, Green.

Cohen, L., Manion, L. and Morrison, K. (2017) *Research Methods in Education.* Abingdon: Routledge.

Cottrell, S. (2008) *The Study Skills Handbook* (4th edn.). Basingstoke: Palgrave Macmillan.

Creme, P. and Lea, M. (2008) *Writing at University: A Guide for Students* (3rd edn). Maidenhead: Open University Press.

Crowley, C., Hallam, S., Hare, R. and Lunt, I. (2003) 'Peer support for people with same-sex attraction', in Nind, M., Sheehy, K. and Simmons, K. (eds) *Inclusive Education: Learners and Learning Contexts.* London: David Fulton Publishers.

Dearden, C. and Becker, S. (2002) *Young Carers and Education.* Retrieved from: http://ycrg.org.uk/youngCarersDownload/yceduc%5B1%5D.pdf Last accessed 09/05/2018.

Dewey, J. (1933) *How We Think.* Boston, MA: D C Heath and Co.

Farhat, G., Bingham, J., Caulfield, J. and Grieve, S. (2017) 'The academies project: Widening access and smoothing transitions for secondary school pupils to university, college and employment', *Journal of Perspectives in Applied Academic Practice*, Vol. 5, No. 1, pp. 23–30 http://jpaap.napier.ac.uk/index.php/JPAAP/article/view/229/pdf Last accessed 12/05/2017.

Hanscomb, S. (2017) *Critical Thinking: The Basics.* London: Routledge.

Hek, R. (2005) *The Experiences and Needs of Refugee and Asylum Seeking Children in the UK: A Literature Review.* Retrieved from: http://dera.ioe.ac.uk/5398/1/RR635.pdf Last accessed 09/05/2018.

Humphrey, N. and Symes, W. (2010) 'Perceptions of social support and experience of bullying among pupils with autistic spectrum disorders in mainstream secondary schools', *European Journal of Special Needs Education,* Vol. 25, No. 1, pp. 77–91.

Itua, I., Coffey, M., Merryweather, D. and Norton, L. (2014) 'Exploring barriers and solutions to academic writing: Perspectives from students, higher education and further education tutors', *Journal of Further & Higher Education*, Vol. 38, No. 3, pp. 305–326.

Ivanic, R. and Simpson, J. (1992) 'Who's who in academic writing?' In N. Fairclough (Ed.) *Critical Language Awareness.* London: Longman.

Jackson, C. (2006) *'Lads' and 'Ladettes' in School: Gender and a Fear of Failure.* Maidenhead: Open University Press.

Jackson, C. (2013) *Contemporary Debates in the Sociology of Education.* Basingstoke: Palgrave Macmillan, pp. 185–201.

Jalali, R. and Morgan, G. (2018) '"They won't let me back." Comparing student perceptions across primary and secondary Pupil Referral Units', *Emotional and Behavioural Difficulties,* Vol. 23, No. 1, pp. 55–68.

Jewkes, Y. (2004) *Media & Crime: Key Approaches to Criminology.* London: SAGE Publications.

Jobs.ac.uk (no date) *Transferable Skills: The Secret of Success.* Retrieved from: www.jobs.ac.uk/careers-advice/interview-tips/962/transferable-skills-the-secret-of-success Last accessed 09/05/2018.

Kolb, D. (1984) *Experiential Learning as the Science of Learning and Development.* Englewood Cliffs, NJ: Prentice Hall.

Laughey, D. (2009) *Media Studies: Theories and Approaches.* Harpenden: Kamera Books.

Lea, M. (1998) 'Academic literacies and learning in higher education: constructing knowledge through texts and experience', *Studies in the Education of Adults*, Vol. 30, No. 2, pp. 156–171.

Lea, M.R. and Street, B.V. (1998) 'Student writing in higher education: An academic literacies approach', *Studies in Higher Education,* Vol. 23, No. 2, pp. 157–172.

Li, Y., Medwell, J., Wray, D., Wang, L. and Liu, X. (2016) 'Learning styles: A review of validity and usefulness', *Journal of Education and Training Studies,* Vol. 4, No. 10, pp. 90–94.

Lillis, T. (2006) 'Moving towards an 'Academic Literacies' Pedagogy: Dialogues of Participation' in L. Ganobcsik- Williams (ed) *Teaching Academic Writing in UK Higher Education: Theories, Practices and Models.* Basingstoke: Palgrave MacMillan.

Lillis, T. and Turner, J. (2001) 'Student writing in higher education: Contemporary confusion, traditional concerns', *Teaching in Higher Education,* Vol. 6, No. 1, pp. 57–68.

Lowe, H., and Cook, A. (2003) 'Mind the Gap: are students prepared for higher education?', Journal of Further and Higher Education, Vo. 27, No. 1, pp. 53–76.

Magiati, I. and Howlin, P. (2003) 'A pilot evaluation study of the Picture Exchange Communication System (PECS) for children with Autistic Spectrum Disorders', *Autism,* Vol. 7, No. 3, pp. 297–320.

Mercer, N. (2000) *Words and minds: how we use language to think together. London*: Routledge.

Moon, J. (2008) *Critical Thinking: An Exploration of Theory and Practice.* Oxon: Routledge.

Moon, J. (2009) *Achieving Success through Academic Assertiveness.* Oxon: Routledge.

Moon, J. (2010) *A Handbook of Reflective and Experiential Learning: Theory and Practice.* London: Routledge.

Northedge, A. (2003) 'Enabling participation in academic discourse', *Teaching in Higher Education,* Vol. 8, No. 2, pp. 19–180.

Norton, L.S. (1990) 'Essay writing: What really counts?', *Higher Education,* Vol. 20, No. 4, pp. 411–442.

Norton, L.S., Dickins, T.E. and McLaughlin Cook, A.N. (1996a) 'Rules of the game in essay writing', *Psychology Teaching Review,* Vol. 5, No. 1, pp. 1–14.

Norton, L.S., Dickins, T.E. and McLaughlin Cook, A.N. (1996b) 'Coursework assessment: What are tutors really looking for?', in G. Gibbs (ed.) *Improving Student Learning: Using Research to Improve Student Learning.* Oxford: The Oxford Centre for Staff Development, pp. 155–166.

Norton, L. and Pitt, E. with Harrington, K. Elander, J. and Reddy, P. (2009) *Writing Essays @ University: A Guide for Students by Students.* WriteNow CETL. London: Metropolitan University.

QAA (Quality Assurance Agency) (2015) *Subject Benchmark Statement: Education Studies.* Retrieved from: www.qaa.ac.uk/en/Publications/Documents/SBS-education-studies-15.pdf Last accessed 09/05/2018.

Reay, D. and Wiliam, D. (1999) '"I'll be a nothing": Structure, agency and the construction of identity through assessment [1]', *British Educational Research Journal,* Vol. 25, No. 3, pp. 343–353.

Riddick, B. (2012) 'Labelling learners with "SEND": The good, the bad and the ugly', in Armstrong, D. and Squires, G. (eds) *Contemporary Issues in Special Educational Needs*. Berkshire: Oxford University Press and McGraw-Hill Education.

Rivers, I. and Cowie, H. (2006) 'Bullying and homophobia in UK schools: A perspective on factors affecting resilience and recovery', *Journal of Gay & Lesbian Issues in Education*, Vol. 3, No. 4, pp. 11–43.

Rowley, E., Chandler, S., Baird, G., Simonoff, E., Pickles, A., Loucas, T. and Charman, T. (2012) 'The experience of friendship, victimization and bullying in children with an autism spectrum disorder: Associations with child characteristics and school placement', *Research in Autism Spectrum Disorders*, Vol. 6, No. 3, pp. 1126–1134.

Schon, D. (1983) *The Reflective Practitioner*. San Francisco, CA: Jossey-Bass.

Sharp, J. (2009) *Success with your Education Research Project*. Exeter: Learning Matters.

Sommerville, E.M. & Creme, P. (2005). '"Asking Pompeii questions": A cooperative approach to Writing in the Disciplines.' *Teaching in Higher Education*, Vol. 10 pp. 17–28.

Target Jobs www.targetjobs.co.uk Last accessed 09/05/2018.

The Open University, *Advanced Evaluation Using PROMPT*. Retrieved from: www.open.ac.uk/libraryservices/documents/advanced-evaluation-using-prompt.pdf Last accessed 09/05/2018.

Thomas, G. (2017) *How to Do Your Research Project*. London: SAGE Publications.

Timmins, S. (2017) *Developing Resilience in Young People with Autism Using Social Stories*. London: Jessica Kingsley Publishers.

UEA (University of East Anglia) (2017a) *Plagiarism and Collusion*. Retrieved from: https://portal.uea.ac.uk/learning-and-teaching/students/advice-on-difficulties/plagiarism-and-collusion?_ga=2.4893684.632770617.1502187800-965106444.1499254854 Last accessed 08/08/2017.

University of Bradford, Academic Skills Advice. PROMPT: Checklist for Quality Sources. Retrieved from: www.bradford.ac.uk/academic-skills/media/academicskillsadvice/documents/academicskillsresources/researchskills/infosheet-PROMPT.pdf Last accessed 09/05/2018.

van Doeselaar, L., Meeus, W., Koot, H.M. and Branje, S. (2016) 'The role of best friends in educational identity formation in adolescence', *Journal of Adolescence*, Vol. 47, pp. 28–37.

Vygotsky, L.S. (1978) *Mind in Society: The Development of Higher Psychological Processes*. Cambridge, MA: Harvard University Press.

Webb, T. (2000) 'Can children with autism be taught to communicate using PECs?', *Good Autism Practice Journal*, Vol. 1, No. 1, pp. 29–42.

Westrup, R. (2009) *Writing Narratives: An exploration of undergraduate students' relationships with essay* writing. Unpublished PhD Thesis. Lancaster University, UK.

Westrup, R. (2017) *Guide to Studying Education*, The Complete University Guide. Retrieved from: www.thecompleteuniversityguide.co.uk/courses/education/guide-to-studying-education/Last accessed 15/08/2018.

Williams, K. (2005) 'Lecturer and first year student (mis)understandings of assessment task verbs: "Mind the gap"', *Teaching in Higher Education*, Vol. 10, No. 2, pp. 157–173.

Wragg, E.C. (1999) *An Introduction to Classroom Observation* (2nd edn). Oxon: Routledge.

Index